Rule of Thirds

Neil Wilkins

Neil Wilkins

Copyright © 2018 Neil Wilkins

All rights reserved.

ISBN: 1719254575
ISBN-13: 978-1719254571

GRATITUDE

I am very grateful to all my clients, colleagues and business partners for their contributions to my thinking and experience, allowing me to test concepts and models with their wonderful products and services.

I'm especially grateful to Charles Nixon, Jim Hardcastle, Karl Meyer and Paul Skuse for the part they have played in the early days of my digital journey, their ideas and thinking and for co-authoring some of my earlier publications and blogs.

Thank you to Dave Ford for his creativity and design.

I dedicate this book to my soul partner Sonya, for her constant love, inspiration, ideas and support; this book would not have been possible without you, my love.

With much gratitude.

Neil Wilkins

CONTENTS

	How to Read This Book	1
1	Plan : Mission	
	1. Focus on Outcomes	5
	2. Build Professional Intimacy	21
	3. Create Advocacy	25
2	Plan : Trends	
	1. Mobility	31
	2. Internet of Things	35
	3. Creating a Community	43
	4. Audio	59
3	Plan : Digital Strategy	
	1. Insights	63
	2. Smart KPIs, Strategy, Plans	71
	3. Internal Communications	77
	4. Return on Investment (ROI)	83
4	Optimise : Personas	
	1. Define, Find and Listen	93
	2. Build Faith and Trust	97
	3. Power of Influencers	101
5	Optimise : Customer Journey	
	1. Build Awareness	103
	2. Convert with Confidence	109
	3. Retain to Sustain your Business	113
6	Optimise : Content Strategy	
	1. Rule of Thirds	117
	2. Become Current, Relevant, Informed	123
	3. Creation, Curation, Documentation	127
7	Deliver : Websites	
	1. Digital Hub	129
	2. Blogs and People	141
	3. Customer and Search Optimisation	149

8	Deliver : Social Media	
	1. From Reactive to Proactive	155
	2. Social Media Guidelines	159
	3. Twitter, Facebook, Linkedin et al	163
9	Deliver : Campaigns	
	1. Paid, Owned, Earned Media	171
	2. Email Marketing	187
10	Improve : Listening	
	1. Google Analytics	193
	2. Social Media Insights	201
	3. Social Listening	207
11	Listening : Share	
	1. Information into Intelligence	211
12	Listening : Innovate	
	1. Customer Relationship Management	221
	2. Adapting Behaviours	225
	3. Leaving a Legacy	231

HOW TO READ THIS BOOK

This book should help you to create great content. Not just good content, all about you, but exceptional and engaging content that inspires, motivates and drives people to doing things.

I have included lots of practical thinking, stories, ideas and checklists to help reinforce your learning.

As you work your way through the book you should read around the subject and collect examples from the real world to help you figure out how everything can be applied in practice, in your unique situation.

I will keep you posted with my observations and insights at www.neilwilkins.online

There are three ways you can use this book.

Power User

As a Power User you can read it from cover to cover and absorb everything at a forensic level. You could read all the stories and forget the theory. The stories are a lighter way of picking up the key points but by limiting yourself solely to these you might miss some useful insights that will take your content to the next level and beyond.

Lite User

As a Lite User it's all about the stories and completing the checklists, so that you glean some knowledge and allow yourself to think, as well as create a plan. You'll create the ultimate in digital content whilst understanding the frameworks behind digital marketing techniques and best practice.

Fast Track User

You could Fast Track through the book by focusing solely on the checklists and if you were to complete those in order then you would have yourself a digital communications plan that could form the basis of a marketing strategy, product launch or propel to the next level, your own personal profile online.

The concepts in this book have been assimilated and developed over a quarter of a century, since I started my digital journey. I have been involved in digital marketing and content creation for as long as I can remember.

Back in 1993 I launched my first website when a web page was as exciting as a plain piece of paper with some writing on it. No images, no interaction, no video, no engagement, just words.

As a marketer I quickly realised that if I could see something on my screen and someone else could see the exact same thing on their computer across the other side of the world, then we could be onto a new way of communicating ourselves, our brands, our products and our services.

Today this may seem blatantly obvious but back in those days we had to drag colleagues, management and clients, kicking and screaming into what seemed to be a brave new world. The number of times I heard the phrase "It'll never catch on". How wrong they were and how in such a short period of time, everything has changed.

It is some thirty years since the birth of the internet and yet many people still use phrases such as "new media", "digital marketing", "e-marketing", "online content" and of course people of all generations still say, "I am not technical". You've heard that and maybe you have said it. Well, the time has long since passed when this is new stuff, when it's technical, when it is out of reach of the vast majority of us on this planet. It is simply how the world communicates and engages.

This is the essence of this book. It is not written to convince you that it's right for you. It is not designed to baffle you, to frighten you away from experimenting, or to leave you feeling inadequate and that everyone else is racing ahead of you.

This book is written with the intention of helping you to relax into a lifelong journey both personally and professionally of understanding how, where and why you could use some carefully selected digital tools and content that you choose from the plethora of those available to help you and maybe your business, engage more effectively and comfortably with those you need to communicate with.

Nothing happened yesterday, nothing will happen today and nothing will happen tomorrow, without connection.

Connection is one of the most significant universal laws that influences and controls how human beings live, think, develop and interact.

Think about the start of your morning.

Perhaps you woke up and checked your smartphone. Your phone was connected to the wall to power the battery overnight as you slept. The phone is now connected to your wifi or cellular network. Your apps and software are connected to servers and databases that in turn connect to your friends', family and colleagues' devices. You connect to your contacts and the connected interactions, digitally or physically, begin.

If your morning began without the ubiquitous checking of email and social media then you may have sat quietly meditating or practicing yoga. Again this is connection, but this time with yourself.

The phrase "humans are social things", is inherently true, even for introverts. The key is understanding and establishing the right balance for the individual at certain times of the day, days of the week, times of the month and perhaps through circadian or lunar cycles and beyond.

Take time to reflect on today's connections: who, what, when and importantly, why.

This is the beginning of your digital content journey because a deep and intimate understanding of the connection and communication preferences of those you wish to engage with are vital to ensure you remain relevant and appropriate in their eyes.

We will explore dialogue as the key to effective digital content. Rather than being about your brand, yourself or your products and services, dialogue is about working with the outcomes that your audience would like to experience. A two way flow of communication in preference to monologue where your only interest is yourself.

1.1 PLAN : MISSION : FOCUS ON OUTCOMES

The last 24 months has seen a significant increase in the range of digital media channels available to the marketer.

It is vital therefore to ensure campaign planning focuses on desired outcomes, target audience and sustainable, relevant engagement rather than simply channels themselves. The digital media channels are tools to be used to enable a consistent and measurable digital journey for the customer, rather than being an end result in themselves.

However, many marketers are swept along in the digital media hype, setting up and devoting precious resources and time in the pursuit of unnecessary activities in channels where their target audience either isn't present or are inactive.

The best starting point in digital media channel selection is to consider whether activities could be owned, earned or paid for.

There may be a balance between all three approaches, smoothly integrating the production of great content, with shareable engagement and topping this up with paid awareness creation to scale up the activities to reach a critical mass of target audience.

However the channels are considered and whichever make the final campaign list, the key current trends for the marketer to focus on include:

- creating a relevant and engaged community
- stimulating advocacy through the channels to maximise impact and reach
- resources available to manage the breadth of channels
- understanding of the required content and media appropriate to each channel

Delivering Value through Digital Marketing and Social Networking

We are often challenged with statements like 'prove to me there's value in spending time in social media' and 'I can't see the point of social networking'.

Rather than wheel out a heavyweight marketing textbook packed with jargon, science and theory we thought it would be helpful to visualise a simple pattern of thinking that can help move your business forward at the same time as ensuring that it develops a key role in its social community.

There is no getting away from it. Every business in every sector is part, whether it wants to be or not, of a social ecosystem. Customers, suppliers, buyers, media and employees are all players in a complex web of digital communication and it often seems difficult to see a link between such communication and business growth.

So here is a simple process that we can call a Digital Strategy to help you focus your time and energy where it really matters, on doing things that will help to deliver increased numbers of profitable, loyal customers and sustained repeat sales.

Step 1 - Set your Goals
Think 3 years ahead and what your business needs to look like and how much revenue you are expecting. What types of customers you will need and how many of them will you need to achieve those goals. Remember, business growth = number of customers x value of sales

Step 2 - Prioritise Profitable Customers
Not all customers are the same. Build really clear profiles of the personas of your most profitable or important customers who will help you to deliver those revenue goals. Really picture them and get to know them, their likes, their needs and not only from a business perspective, think about their interests, their location and the kinds of brands, products and services they like

Step 3 - Build Awareness
You need to find these customers and engage with them through digital tools like website, social media and email. If you know what they are interested in and what they like then talk about that as well as your products and services. This is talking on their terms and they will be more likely to listen. Balance this with a little about you and your business. We call this the rule of thirds (one third about you, one third signposting to things they like, one third about your products and services). Remember to select only the digital tools that these target customers use already. You need

to go and find them where they are rather than expect them to come to you

Step 4 - Conversion

You have those goals to meet so see how many of these newly aware customers you can convert into real paying customers. Use appropriate digital tools to turn their hopes into faith in you and trust in your business or brand. Appropriate tools may be very different to those you used to get their attention when you built their awareness. This difference is what we call the customer journey, a step by step hand-holding of the customer to the point of a confident purchase

Step 5 - Retention

Using the same rule of thirds but maybe different digital tools you take your customers into the retention phase of their customer journey. Encouraging up selling or cross selling of other products and services you begin to generate some real lifetime value from each customer at the same time as building their loyalty. Stay close, give value, remain personally connected and social. They may then become advocates and market on your behalf, encouraging more profitable customers just like them into a customer journey with you

Step 6 - Measure and Improve

Using a digital dashboard like Social Report you can keep a check on how you are doing across all of your digital tools. Make sure you are getting the right message out there, check your customers' interests are what you think they are, make fine tuning updates of content, tools and tone of voice and do more of what's working best and strip out the things that make no difference. This is the point where you'll see if you are getting the revenue you need from the customers you wanted and importantly if those customers are advocating you so that your business and its sales continue to grow towards your goals.

Digital Content and Marketing is more than simply establishing a web site. There is a complex integration of a variety of channels including web sites, e-newsletters, discussion lists, direct email, online PR, social media, affiliate schemes, advertising and sponsorship which together have the capability of moving a business into previously unseen growth.

In designing a digital presence there are a host of

considerations, many of which are common sense and arguably few which actually require detailed technical implementation and skill sets.

User friendliness is key. The aim is to provide a customer experience (UX) which envelops and entices the user. This can be called 'customer journey' a key concept of the flow of experience the customer enjoys as they pass through brands, products and services on their way to an eventual outcome or action.

The origins of the powerful set of online tools we now have at our disposal began when Tim Berners-Lee and colleagues at CERN in Switzerland developed the concept of the world wide web (www).

This allowed much more user-friendly access to the hardware backbone which was the internet, and established the protocol and basic building blocks, like HTML, that allow us to create content in a way that can be read by anyone with a suitable reading programme (browser) anywhere on earth.

It also allowed for development of the plug-ins, graphical and movie content, hypertext links, cookies and all the other characteristics and benefits that we now take for granted in our everyday online activities.

In the 1990s the internet was regarded by some as a fad which would be replaced when the next big thing came along. Others regarded it as a subversive medium which would threaten our society.

But now, in a world with a population of 7.56 billion (source: world-statistics.org) where 2.4bn people will use a smartphone this year, and penetration will continue to increase to, by the end of 2018, more than a third of the global population using a smartphone (source: e-marketer.com); Digital marketing has arrived.

What does success really look like to you?

There is always so much pressure to hit the numbers. Your boss keeps the foot to the pedal and pushes you to do likewise. The cashflow for the end of the month drives you to squeeze every last moment of time and energy into creating enough *revenue to pay the bills that you know are due.*

It is often hard to pause for breath and wonder what it's all worth. So today, for a moment, do just that.

Take half an hour out of your day and perhaps as you read this, step away from email and the phone and go to a quiet place where you won't be interrupted.

In this pause, begin to think about what success really looks like. It is very unlikely to be the money you are generating or the project you are completing, the noise you are making or the people you are influencing.

It is far more likely to be a vision on the horizon that looks, sounds and importantly, feels, better than the situation you have today.

So get this vision of success in your mind's eye and really feel what it's like to have already achieved it. How does it make you feel? Not how does it look or how does it sound, but how does it make you feel.

Those who focus on Vision, Clarity and Purpose and how their end goal feels, are significantly more likely to achieve, because they have already psychologically committed to doing everything possible in its pursuit.

Once you have embedded the feeling you can set about creating SMART (specific, measurable, achievable, realistic, time-bound) step-by-step milestones for the journey to achieving it.

And when you have done that you can return to the email inbox and voicemails that you have just avoided, confident in the knowledge that your subconscious mind will ensure you are now focusing only on what really makes a difference.

Digital marketing, or for some, simply 'marketing', provides an unprecedented growth opportunity for individuals, and businesses large and small. It allows organisations theoretically to achieve a global reach to new customers and for competitors to do the same.

With such a mass of communication and the corresponding

rapid growth of data centers, many deep under the deserts of our world, we are already consumed by digital chaos, often to the point where as customers we simply don't know who to trust or where to look next. Retaining our privacy as we move around the digital space is a concern for many whilst balancing freedom of speech and our desire to cultivate our own digital personas to compliment our busy lifestyles.

With opportunity comes challenges and this study guide is designed to focus on the key building blocks that today's marketer needs to focus on to provide value-rich communications to our most profitable and valuable customers.

The Importance of a Vision Statement

In marketing, business creation and development and sales, it's vital to have a clear company vision. This is different to your mission statement and here's why…

The mission statement is a collective agreement of operationally, what everyone will do together. It is akin to being 'on a mission' so to speak. An action-oriented set of aims, that encourage those in the organisation to operate as a team.

The company vision is a higher level collective intention. Rather than operational it is aspirational and a collective feeling of how the world will look different as the organisation achieves its goals.
In many ways it is not possible to create a strategic business plan without either of the vision or mission statements because together they set a guiding light from which the organisation's objectives can be set.

There's something really clean, crips and clear about a well crafted vision.

A vision is important if you want to enjoy true purpose, consistent and focused intention and at the same time, take a path towards achieving it.

We all know people who have the next big dream. They may even create a plan around that dream. They have intention and desire, they share it with everyone and they may really believe it's both achievable and realistic.

In many cases though they may lack a true vision. As time passes and they take their route map towards achieving their dream, things may cloud, they may lose focus or tire as pressures of every day living take their toll.

So we focus on the importance of vision. By vision we mean "the faculty or state of being able to see" and "the ability to think about or plan the future with imagination or wisdom." (Google Search)

These definitions bring about synonyms: imagination, creativity, creative power, inventiveness, innovation, inspiration, intuition, perceptiveness, perception, breadth of view, foresight, insight, far-sightedness, prescience, discernment, awareness, penetration, shrewdness, sharpness, cleverness. So vision is focus in all its traditional meanings. Using the five senses to virtually experience what it'll be like when the vision is realised and it materialises in front of you.

But there's more. Great minds tell us that there are more than our well known five senses, there is feeling, intuition, intellect and our soul.

Taking feeling and intuition, a true vision is something that will permeate every fibre of our body, every moment of our waking life. An obsession if you like, in a very positive sense.

If we have a vision that represents our chosen future reality we can begin to introduce examples of best practice and people who match at least part of our ideal. Continuous personal development and a thirst of self improvement and learning is at the heart of successfully achieving a vision. For example, speakers can speak but not necessarily present, so they learn. Salespeople can sell but without an ideal specification of the ultimate salesperson, how can they know what's best practice and how to turn their potential into reality.

The clearer the vision the more obvious the skills, support, learning and experience we need to fold into our lives to take us step and step towards our ultimate destination.

Everything we are experiencing today is feeding tomorrow's internet cloud, the virtual space from where tomorrow's social networking, search and online marketing will be driven.

When looking at the specific tools of digital marketing it is important to remember the marketing context and the fundamentals of the Marketing Mix. The marketing mix originally consisted of 4Ps: Product, Price, Place and Promotion. These were originally used to structure marketers' thinking to ensure no stone was left unturned when planning.

This was fine in the days when marketing was concerned with the marketing of physical products, as was the case for most of the period up until the late 1970s. However with the inexorable growth of the service sector the 4Ps were no longer sufficient. We needed to take account of the 'people' aspect of service and the process by which customers enquired and bought the service.

In addition given the very limited physicality of a service we needed to give greater emphasis to the packaging or physical elements. Consequently, People, Process and Physical Evidence were added to the marketing mix giving us the 7Ps, each of which has a digital aspect.

Subsequently the mix grew to 10Ps in order to be more explicit about the role of stakeholders: Public opinion which explicitly takes into account the issue of social media; Political power and regulatory control, especially with the issue of internet privacy; and Partners and stakeholders.

So now, when considering each of the elements of the marketing mix, we need to bear in mind that they must not be considered in isolation. They need to be considered as a coordinated set of tools, any one of which will influence the others.

When introducing a new product, for example, it is important to consider the pricing and the distribution of that product. If the market is not aware of it then the product will not be successful so promotion is essential. Coordination and integration of messages and channels are therefore important elements in all marketers' tool kits and as you work through the marketing mix you always need to consider how each element can impact on the others.

Get a Grip of Your Marketing

In today's increasingly competitive marketplace and with the uncertainties of the impact of Brexit and continued global financial and political turbulence, it's vital to continually assess and improve your marketing development.

Here are 9 of the key elements that you should be continuously reviewing and integrating into your monthly, quarterly and annual business reviews (and if you don't currently conduct such reviews, then that's a mother conversation we should have!):

Insights - Constantly look for significant trends in technology, competitor performance, customer preferences and new product and market opportunities

Strategy - Determine exactly what your Unique Sales Proposition is and continuously review it to ensure that it is genuinely unique. This is your core competence that competitors can't emulate and as such it should be at the centre of your marketing and sales communications

Customer Voice - Always be listening to your most profitable and value customer personas. These are the customers who's voice you must reflect back into your organisation so that you are continuously providing products, services and marketing messages to them that enable them to perceive the great value that you are adding to their world

Brand - Remember that your people, as well as your company style, tone of voice, logo and digital footprint, should be at the centre of your brand. Everyone in your firm has a part to play in appropriately conveying the value you are adding to the customers' experience

Integration - Joining up all of your marketing is key to both being able to measure the effectiveness as well as providing a consistent customer journey. Regular review of the appropriateness and performance of all marketing tools is vital to keep the journey relevant and the marketing resources efficient

Digital - Leading on from the integration, with the proliferation of new digital technologies, social media platforms and devices, it's all about prioritising what's relevant as communication channels from your customers' perspective rather than simply jumping on each and every new opportunity

Proposition - Always a key element in the marketing

communications mix, your core proposition (sometimes called a strapline) must continuously reflect the perceived value the customers seek. if it isn't, and you will likely need to be constantly asking them, then it's time for either a rebrand, some fine tuning and perhaps a full customer research or satisfaction survey

Partners - As the world becomes ever-more interconnected, the opportunities for collaboration, association and partnership cannot be ignored in the most progressive of organisations. How are you currently and in the future, planning on being accessible and responsive to partnership opportunities?

Metrics - ROI is at the heart of effective sales, marketing and business management. A key part of each and every review meeting should be your dashboard, a means of watching and responding to even the most subtle of observable trends.

Promotion is a range of tools that need to be selected and coordinated appropriately, all within the context of the wider Marketing Mix. The Promotions or Communications Mix includes not only the type of communication to be used but also selection of the right media.

With media comes content, the fuel of the channels in which it is published.

Also, are you going to use a mix of offline and online marketing channels and tools? It is highly likely that you will throughout your customers' journey need to integrate both offline and online tools. Even in heavily online biased examples like an e-commerce store, there is often a physical product arriving on the doorstep and as such that is still part of the customers' journey.

Digital communications includes the aspect of dialogue. Historically most marketing communications were one way, but with the arrival of social media, there is a two-way dialogue, a conversation, which needs to be stimulated and managed by the organisation.

A Rebrand isn't just a New Logo

Marketing and Rebranding is more than just the veneer of a new colour scheme, font or logo. A true rebrand is a complete re-invention of the business. It's underpinned by a new structure, *development opportunities realised, team skills enhanced and increased customer intimacy and feedback loops.*

A rebrand is a great opportunity to truly take stock of all the innovations and opportunities that have been presented to the business in recent years. Prioritise them and decide which add value in the short term and which add value in the longer term. From there it's a case of allocation of roles. Everyone needs to take responsibility and ownership for at least one element of improvement that is going to happen. In this way there is a wider collective buy-in and the reason and philosophy behind the rebrand will become self-evident for all.

The exercise isn't a one-time-only job, it's the start of an ongoing journey of listening to customers and staff and reprioritising the very best innovations, ideas and suggestions which are then incorporated within the new brand structure.

For clarity and as a filter for what's right and wrong, what's important and what's less so, are the leading lights of the vision and mission statement. These should always be clear and directional for the brand and under which all of the supporting elements of business process, people, systems and customer service are positioned.

If your business is ready for growth, to enter new markets, to launch new products and services, then there is also an opportunity for a rebrand and the wider business improvements that underpin it.

The product element of the marketing mix has arguably had the greatest overhaul as a result of the digital age.

Whilst physical products are still manufactured and distributed much of the economy is now service based and can be digitised. In addition, many of what were seen as physical products have also been digitised causing a reinvention of for example, the music industry and in publishing.

The creation of the App (mobile application software) has created a world where almost any product benefit that can be digitised, will be. From just 500 Apps in 2007 when the iTunes App store opened there are now over half a million Apps and 50 billion downloads with nearly as many Android downloads too.

The strategic issues facing marketers will continue to include product definition, selection of range width and depth, brand building, management of the wider product portfolio and control and development of the perception of quality within the overall product strategy, especially when digitisation results in commoditisation and the threat of reduced prices.

With availability of information through digital media, comes the customer expectation of wider choice, availability and immediacy of delivery. This places significant challenges on today's marketer who will continuously need to seek better and more efficient ways of serving the customer.

A great example of this comes in the form of self-service. In the past, products needed to be delivered physically but with the arrival of 3D printing, a customer has the potential (depending on the product of course) to download the design template and produce/print the product locally. This can save considerable time and cost and provide the digital marketer with a significant opportunity to scale their product delivery internationally and at the customers' convenience.

People are still a key consideration in the marketing mix. Organisations must consider if they have the experience internally to plan and deliver digital and social networking activity. If not then some integration of third party specialists and agencies may be required for the initial research, auditing and planning as well as the ongoing delivery of campaigns and supporting tactical activity.

In digital, people are even more critical to good online customer service and constant monitoring of people by people is essential to ensure that conversations, especially in social media, are choreographed and negative publicity carefully managed.

When in an online space, all organisations operate on a 24/7, 365 days a year basis. The online experience never sleeps and as such organisations must prepare to deliver a consistent service, often irrespective of from where in the world the visitor or customer is making contact.

This becomes particularly important when you consider that not all working weeks are Monday to Friday 9-5. In the Gulf States for example, the traditional working week is Sunday to Thursday. It goes without saying that organisations in the Far East are operating on very different geographic time zones to those in the Far West.

For many businesses, the promotion of their place is integral to the value and perception in the eyes of their customer. Made in Britain, for example still has a value of high quality and tradition, for those in overseas markets. If you are located in a specific city or region that is inherent in your brand values or expected geography of your product or service then this can be built into the digital marketing mix.

Google itself rewards companies who consistently share the geographic locations of their offices, outlets and people, with more precise search engine results rankings. Location will continue to feature as a key element in the digital marketing mix.

By including real world geography (country name, city name, region, zip code or post code) in digital content, search engine optimisation (SEO) can be enhanced for searches that are localised.

As more and more digital access to the internet is via mobile devices (smartphones, wearable devices and tablets) that know where they are, the linking of device/user with their physical location enables more highly relevant search results to be presented to them.

Brands that are most easily found are now including location at the core of their content strategy through both their websites and social media accounts.

Process is now critical in the way potential and returning customers can navigate around your website(s), be able to purchase or find information and share it with others.

This leads to a consideration of the back office systems and processes in a language and on terms appropriate to the customer. If, as is the case with most organisations, English is the predominant first online language, it is strategically important to consider how this might impact the customer experience if a priority target country or region does not have English, or the English alphabet, as a regularly used and acceptable language.

The choice of third party websites and social networking platforms is also an important consideration. The assumption of dominance of Facebook, Twitter and LinkedIn, may or may not be applicable to some target countries where locally popular social networks are significant. Examples of this can be seen in Germany, China, Italy and Brazil where locally popular variants of the 'Big 3' are present and dominant.

When planning to serve more than your local area or region it is very important to consider how customer service will be provided. Without a physical presence in a particular place there has to be a greater reliance on third party support and delivery services and an extension of the traditional supply chain as well as after-sales service. In this instance the careful selection of online messages and levels of promise must be in line with the digital promises and marketing to ensure the customer perceives the value of the promise in line with the actual experience received.

The broader the range of regions and countries served online, the wider the potential range of marketing, products and services required. The assumption that new regions will accept the existing way of marketing and doing business may not be valid.

Local product and service variants as well as website styles and tuning of digital marketing activity may be necessary.

Pricing concepts have had to be adapted to the internet as the concept of free content has permeated much of what is 'for sale' on the internet. Software, services and support are often offered free at point of purchase but paid for either through advertising or through upgrades. Price comparison is also so much easier online.

Pricing can be a sensitive issue across international borders and the complexity of online legislation, regulations and local tax implications will all affect how organisations can do business.

There is also the opportunity to develop bespoke cost and pricing models throughout the supply chain with extranets opening up the chance to allow password access to restricted sites and bespoke price lists and product groups as appropriate.

Pricing online is not always simple. There can be issues of transparency across borders, across markets and across customer segments. There is not always a requirement for the organisation to supply outside of its territory but this needs to be clearly communicated at point of purchase or before.

Price is a very important element of the digital marketing mix. Prices in some categories (books and music) have dropped by up to 40% in recent years and in the online marketplace pricing is now used as a competitive differentiation tool. However, the challenge faced by all companies is not to over-utilise pricing and thereby drive down overall market value and threaten margins across each industry. Pricing must be in line and consistent with other elements of the marketing mix and of course the brand value and position.

In close association with pricing is costing. Amazon for instance have set out with the objective to control their entire supply chain by establishing a highly focused cost model based on low overhead and logistic/supply chain. Dell, in a not dissimilar manner continue to operate around 10% below average industry costs, in part due to their focus on direct selling through the internet in preference to the more typical reseller supply chain model.

The customer expectations of 'a good deal' in online pricing, have seen a surge in popularity. The availability of voucher sites and cash-back discounts are now expected and the transparency of pricing has resulted in highly competitive situations in many markets.

This downward pressure on pricing forces the marketer into cost and efficiency savings to maintain margins at acceptable levels. Marketers are also on the look-out for new revenue streams to compensate.

Popular websites and social media accounts can now utilise affiliate marketing schemes (the selling of real estate on their websites and in their social media accounts) if their visitor numbers or follower volumes are substantial. When someone purchases another company product having clicked on an affiliate advertisement on the marketer's website, the marketer gains a small commission. At scale, these affiliate advertisements can become an incremental revenue channel, previously not part of the marketing mix.

Physical evidence can be taken as referring to the customers' experience of accessing a website, including navigation, ease of use, value of content and overall 'stickiness'. Products bought online will mostly still require physical delivery for which the brand owner is still responsible, even if the initial transaction was made virtually. A joined up approach is required.

Some businesses have taken the physical evidence to the next level by focusing on the offline delivery and packaging experience as a differentiator in the online sales process. Apple and moo.com packaging for example far outshines the competition at the point the customer receives their online order. The physical element of the customer journey continues far beyond the online experience and marketers must remember to ensure the journey is considered in full.

Checklist : Focus on outcomes

Thinking about your own outcomes, what are your highest level professional goals?

List the barriers or weaknesses that are inhibiting your progress towards your professional goals?

How do you want to be perceived when successful?

What is your most important short term, medium term and long term goal?

Thinking about your customers, how will their world be different when they have a professionally intimate relationship with you?

Rather than marketing product features and benefits, what outcomes will you communicate to your target customers?

How will you know that your customers are perceiving exceptional outcomes from engaging with you?

1.2 PLAN : MISSION : BUILD PROFESSIONAL INTIMACY

Relevance is an essential ingredient in the mix. Companies can no longer publish what they want to say. Instead, they need to understand and publish what their customers want to hear. This is a small but crucial turnaround in emphasis, that makes a fundamental difference to the way brands, products and services are perceived.

Relevance is all about making it personal, customised, even to the point of bespoke, where the customer's perception is that everything they see, read and hear feels as though it was created just for them. At this point, the engagement becomes not only a one-to-one between the organisation and its customers, but beyond to the customers' network of friends, family and colleagues as advocacy, sharing, and even viral, begins to take effect.

Relevance is your customers' perceived connection with what you are saying to a point where psychologically, they accept and engage both practically and emotionally, with your communication.

For example if you are blogging, your customer is looking for you to show evidence that you are current, relevant and informed. Current because they may hear something from you before they hear it from anywhere else. Relevant because it resonates with a need they are trying to resolve or a desire they have for a potential outcome, and relevant because it's all about them. Informed because you are adding additional value to something they may not fully understand.

In blogging, a good example is a review of a service or product offered by a number of companies. If the product category is of interest to your customer and you are providing insight, intelligence and opinion then you are more relevant than simply providing a table of links where they need to self-serve to make comparisons of the products available.

Published interviews are another good example, where people read insightful commentary and informative ideas about a particular subject. That the interviewee is not a celebrity is irrelevant if they are well respected, connected and qualified in the topic being debated.

Humans are curious and enjoy, especially in social media, researching, watching and listening. Relevance is about being in their space, adding value to their world, in a timely, considered and non-intrusive manner.

For centuries, the role of the marketer had been to promote and sell the virtues of their products and services. It is only in the last decade that relevance has become one of the key ingredients in the marketers' recipe book.

Identifying Strengths

Creation of value is everything, both in developing your career, but also more widely in creating sustainable and satisfying professional and personal relationships to support your business growth.

Such value comes in all sorts of guises and one of the most important things you can do when building a successful career plan and business, is to consider where you add most value. To do this effectively you need to be open and honest with yourself and identify your top three strengths.

If you could only provide one skill or experience to work colleagues, business partners or clients, what would it be?

What things about you intrigue other people the most? What subject do people most regularly ask you about? It's likely to indicate the strength or attribute with which they believe you add most value.

What do others say or have said about you in the past? These are all useful tools in identifying your strengths. The strengths you believe you offer may not be the same as those being received.

Be really specific too. Saying "I am good at marketing" won't really help you to build a clearly defined and practical plan. Break down a strength like 'marketing' into its constituent parts and identify which elements you are strongest in. Another example might be a personality trait. Instead of simply saying "I am a good listener", what positive effects does this have on others and what particular things inside being a good listener are you able to identify?

Think also about the things you do in a working day. Which things come naturally, just flow and you enjoy the most? One of your strengths may lie inside how and why you find these things most pleasurable and straightforward to deliver.

Strengths are just one small part of the overall personal career plan and to facilitate business growth and whilst many people think these are the most important elements, they are simply a reflection of where you may add most value.

Checklist : Build professional intimacy

What does professional intimacy look and feel like to you?

How will you know when you have fostered intimate professional relationships?

Where can you find great examples of exceptional customer relationships in your industry or elsewhere?

What will you do to ensure everyone involved in your business understands the importance of customer relationships?

What are the next steps you are going to take today to begin fostering a more professionally intimate business environment?

1.3 PLAN : MISSION : CREATE ADVOCACY

Loyalty can be defined as a strong feeling of allegiance and support.

In digital marketing, customer loyalty is a worthy strategic goal which may in turn give rise to improved and sustainable customer lifetime value. Loyal customers return time and again for repeat purchases, allowing the marketer to up-sell and cross-sell related products and services.

Loyal customers also provide ongoing feedback and ideas for new product development. They are also vocal in their peer communities, as advocates of the brand, and can often come to the support of the organisation when there are online dissenters.

Loyalty is a strategic focus that can feed into tactical social networking and in the creation of effective virtual communities as the most loyal become highly influential in discussions.

Your people are potential marketers and advocates for your brand as much, if not more than your customers. They have a vested interest in sharing the good messages about your products and services and this should be choreographed and encouraged.

Advocacy can be the most powerful form of online marketing, providing the highest returns of value if you harness it.

Advocacy is the sharing of messages, conversations, branding and outcomes by customers with their networks and can result in up to ten times more effectiveness and eventual product purchase than a direct contact with the same organisation. Advocacy is now the staple diet of the strategic digital marketer seeking to ensure that everything they publish from blogs and vlogs to tweets, and e-newsletters to case studies, goes viral and spreads well beyond their first tier of contacts.

Word of mouth (WOM) from which advocacy develops, is not a new concept. It refers to any interpersonal communications which the receiver views as impartial. In essence it is as simple as a colleague coming into work and telling the team that the film they saw last night was excellent and well worth going to see.

WOM can be positive or negative. Indeed the challenge for the marketer is two-fold: how to manage and capitalise on positive WOM and how to minimise negative WOM.

The term 'Viral Marketing' was first coined in 1997 by Steve Jurvetson and Tim Draper. Since its introduction, it has become synonymous for an amplified version of word of mouth. Viral marketing can be defined as making a piece of digital content into a form of advocacy or word of mouth referral endorsement from one client to other prospective clients. It is important to note that WOM still exists independently of the internet.

Viral marketing has developed in an unplanned fashion predominantly through the use of e-mail and social media due to its simplicity, ubiquity and because the communication is free and requires no particular effort by the sender, unlike traditional postal mail or telephone. Viral marketing now encompasses a number of technologies and marketers can benefit from the low cost and potentially wide reach of viral messaging. However a key hurdle is finding a subject that is humorous, fascinating or controversial enough to be worth recipients passing it on. I

Too many agencies and marketers begin with the assumption that they are creating a viral campaign. It is not possible to design a 'Viral Campaign'. A campaign simply goes viral if it's good enough.

Top Tips for Becoming a Digital Extrovert

Being an extrovert using digital communications such as social networking is not about making noise for the sake of noise. It's not about being all me, me, me and it's not about being omnipresent across every single medium. In fact, contrary to popular belief the term extrovert is defined as someone who takes and gives energy from the interaction with others. The converse is the introvert who is happy to self-power their life.

So with this new-found definition there is an opportunity to shape your digital activity to position yourself as current, relevant and informed in the eyes of those with whom you wish to engage. Appropriate and relevant dialogue is the name of the game for the digital extrovert, the person who you first think of when it comes to asking advice and sharing knowledge and information.

The digital extrovert balances their conversations (and notice these are conversations rather than monologues) by sharing information about themselves, by signposting others to things they found interesting in their online travels, and of course using the rule of thirds they overtly share, as the final third, value messages about their products and services.

For the digital extrovert it's fine overtly promoting their products and services because this is acceptable and expected by their audience as they have already engaged with valuable insight and objective information that has enhanced both their relationships but their audiences' lives, both professional and personal.

It is never about me, me, me and it's not about copy and paste. The best digital extroverts take that little extra time to fine tune the messages they share through the various social networks because they understand that whilst the core of the message might be the same, their target audience is either different in each social network or the same but in a different frame of mind when they use each. Take for example Facebook versus Linkedin. It may be that a target audience is using Facebook for personal networking and Linkedin for professional. However this is a sweeping assumption and becoming less relevant by the day.

Far better to really look into your social networks and understand exactly how each group of target audiences is using the network, when, how and why. This insight by group of targets helps the digital extrovert to build and use a clear mental picture of the personas they are talking to in each network and then fine tune the message to them accordingly. One size doesn't fit all. The most successful social networkers are very in tune with the subtle dynamics of their social media, using digital dashboards like SocialReport or SproutSocial to gauge not only connections and their activities but down to fine detail like their interests, their second tier of connections and time of day preferences.

By responding on the terms of the people you are trying to influence and engage with you become socially extrovert, getting what you give on the basis that you reap what you sow and ending sentences and statements with an inviting question mark rather than a full stop. The theory is simple, the practice is just that... by practicing.

Top Tips:

- *Remember it's Research as well as Promotion*
- *Plot Customer Journeys for Priority Personas*
- *Align Activity with Strategic Goals*
- *Balance Awareness, Conversion, Retention*
- *Start Writing Relevant Content*
- *Remember to be Current, Relevant, Informed*
- *Schedule Regular Time to Publish and to Measure*
- *Think Conversations not Monologues*
- *Fine Tune and Re-prioritise*

Share the Success of your Digital Extroversion

Hope Faith and Trust in Social Media Advocacy

It's a commonly known fact that the best results in marketing campaigns, business development and sales processes come when you have been introduced, recommended or advocated by a colleague or friend.

It should come as no surprise then that word of mouth, be it face to face or more likely nowadays through social networks, can produce some of the best return on investment of your time and energy in your marketing, communications and sales efforts.

The reason for this is through the long-held belief that people buy from people rather than buying for product features and benefits. The latter just happens to be a positive by-product from the sales and marketing transaction.

90% of the buying decision comes from whether a person likes the brand or sales person. So why is this word of mouth advocacy so effective?

Well, it's because of the Hope, Faith, Trust model. The buyer firstly has hope they can find a solution to their problem or need. Secondly when they engage with you and your marketing or first touch points in the sales process they gain faith that you will solve this problem or need. Then as they get deeper into the engagement they gain trust that you will deliver the value they are seeking.

The great thing about advocacy and it seems particularly social media advocacy where it's all done in public, is that 80% of the Hope, Faith, Trust journey is completed by the recommendation. In other words they are almost at the point where the buying decision is made, even before you have met them or they have personally engaged with you, your brand, your products or services.

Social advocacy and word of mouth should therefore form a core part of your marketing strategy, whatever you are selling.

Checklist : Create advocacy

Who would you like to become advocates of your business?

What does advocacy look like to you?

How will you know when you have advocates?

Do you have current examples of advocates?

What will happen when your advocates are advocating (more)?

What are you going to do today to increase the chances that your existing customers advocate you (more)?

2.1 PLAN : TRENDS : MOBILITY

As relevance becomes central to marketing thinking when considering the customer, we need to look deeply into the changes and trends in their behaviour. By knowing where their worlds are heading and their preferences in behaviour we can adapt the timing, precision and delivery of our marketing communications to ensure our targeting hits the right spot.

With this in mind, a key trend is mobility.

It is no coincidence that as more and more people use their mobile devices (smartphones, tablets, watches) for digital communication they become less and less tethered to a physical location.

This has the benefit of freedom and flexibility and offers up numerous advantages to the savvy marketer who can dovetail their customer journey in time and place with their target customer's world.

We have seen an upturn in the impact and importance of mobile access where visitors to websites and social networks engage at a time and place to suit them rather than waiting until returning to office or home to go online.

Most social networks now attempt to bridge the gap between the online world and real world.

The revolution taking place in marketing has been propelled by technology and is affecting all aspects of the marketing discipline so no practitioner can afford to overlook the frequency of changes taking place and the level of attention to detail required for efficiency.

At the centre of this digital marketing revolution is Web 2.0, a concept of understanding and relating to the web whereby the rules by which business is conducted is different, as users add value to the webbed network via the platforms from which they gain access to the internet. Blogging or Blogs is an off shoot of this digital revolution that has been going from strength to strength. Research by LearnHub showed that 22 of the most popular websites in the world are Blogging websites.

Not only is the mobile customer able to interact digitally from wherever they are but the marketer is able to publish, blog and vlog remotely at a time and place that suits them. Nobody is office or home bound when it comes to digital.

An outcome of this trend towards mobility is that marketers now need to consider mobile first in their marketing planning. In simple terms this means that website design should originate from the most popular browser and backfill others in support. When mobile internet access overtook fixed location access for the first time in 2017 the need to design a digital customer experience from first considering mobile access was assured.

The first consideration of this type is the size of screen. The phrase 'a picture tells a thousand words' becomes poignant with limited screen space in which to convey messages.

Secondly it is speed of access. Whilst wifi remains the preferred connection choice for most, 3G and 4G access is not omnipresent and so those who design fast, minimalist and effective experiences for their audiences are those who will win the battle of keeping customers satisfied. We all have limited attention spans and within the mobile space this is even more poignant.

Thirdly the mobile device is most often 'always on', even at night time when the customer is sleeping. With an ever-present channel from marketer to customer competitors vie for the customer's attention creating a chaotic melee of sound, images and video. The winners are the marketers who listen and understand exactly when the customer is most receptive to hearing from them.

The basics of marketing where experience should be on the terms of the customer, apply more in mobile marketing than ever. As a customer, if you fit in around my busy lifestyle and cut through the noise, I am far more likely to listen, engage and respond. If you market to me when it's convenient to you then I am hearing your messages along with your competitors and it's all too much and inconvenient for me.

The mobile landscape is constantly evolving. New smart devices with easy to use software and creative tariffs from the mobile networks are encouraging people of all ages to use more of their functionality from music, video and pictures to email communications and GPS mapping on the move.

The mobile device has of course evolved far beyond simple voice and text messaging; it sits at the centre of our lives at home and at work. Text messaging (SMS) and instant messaging remain a strong story. It is currently an integral part of our lifestyle and has shown good growth as sending messages between mobile devices has become an essential part of everyday life for many people.

Checklist : Mobility

How do you currently respond to the mobile opportunity?

What have you learned from the trend of mobility?

What are your competitors doing with mobility?

What will you do differently today, to respond to the mobility opportunity?

How will you keep abreast of other trends related to mobility?

2.2 PLAN : TRENDS : INTERNET OF THINGS

Data has win-win benefits in both the direction of the customer as well as the organisation.

As data capture and usage grows exponentially year on year, we see huge opportunities to fine tune customer experiences and the provision of services digitally.

As the customer shares their personal details, location, product usage, preferences and feedback, the organisation can collect (as far as GDPR regulations permit, in Europe) and interpret this information and turn it into intelligence.

The intelligence informs better decision making, opportunities for new product and service development and improvement in ways of working and communicating. In turn, these innovations benefit the customer.

As the customer then becomes more confident in transacting with the organisation they communicate more frequently, more openly and help to improve the intimacy of the relationship. This provides value and sustainability in the relationship on both sides and enhances the customers' lifetime value.

Digital marketers are well positioned to put data at the heart of their strategy and tactical plans to ensure they have evidence for their return on investment in time and resources.

There is still a debate about whether cloud marketing and the next generation of the web will be driven by search. The current search model in digital marketing assumes the user has most control. They know what they are looking for as they input their key word or long tail phrase into their trusted search engine. Out pops the search engine result, a list of organic results based on the quality of web page the engine assumes will be of value to you and a host of sponsored links where those vying for your valuable attention bid for space to be seen before their competitors.

It is a simple and proven model that works a treat for all concerned and generates billions of dollars each year for content providers, engines, brokers, advertisers and wholesalers.

So will this be the logical model that cloud marketing will evolve from? That would be an evolution but in some ways a shame because it misses an opportunity for cloud marketing to create its own revolution, putting the driving force not in the hands of a searching user but in the relevant situation in which they find themselves bringing into play location, purchase history, activity and 'likes'...

Everything Appropriate, Everywhere I Need It

The more Big Data infiltrates cloud computing, cloud marketing and social media the more there is a danger we are proliferating one of the most annoying elements of our connected world.

Social media, online advertising, integrated digital TV experiences, the noise and chatter of content, interaction and communication is everywhere.

As we enjoy the benefits of blanket wifi coverage in cities, superfast broadband in rural areas and the likely next iteration of web services in what I have been calling Cloud Marketing for a couple of years, we may also see simply too much noise and herein lies our challenge.

There are numerous benefits of living in a fully connected world with data and content empowering us anytime, any place. But there will be times, and in fact probably most of the time, when we want to carefully filter out extraneous noise to be able to focus on what's really important and relevant and what truly adds value to our real lives.

Everything Everywhere is an interesting brand position because in many ways it introduces the idea of empowerment. You can have everything everywhere but in fact that's just potential. What we really need is everything appropriate, everywhere we need it. In that way we can fuse digital experiences and especially those through our mobile devices, with the different needs that we have at different times of the day and in different physical places, and these all based on our chosen privacy settings and personal preferences.

For the marketer of the (near) future it will be all about a *detailed understanding of the needs and desires of the customer so that they are able to fine tune their messages, not to overload, and to ensure that timing and relevance are factored into all communication.*

Do you have this level of understanding of your customers? Now would be a good time to begin...

Google's algorithms already take into account many known and unknown factors but one which appears to be gaining in significance is the power of location. As Google builds it's semantic web, where each crawl through each website helps it to organically learn the context, relevance and importance of the page against the potential visitors' interest in it, we will see more and more weight placed on location.

For the marketer this means consistently and constantly adding in physical or geographic location, again providing more of a bridge between real and online worlds. As an example if you open your browser in London and search for a local pizza restaurant you will see a very different local result than when you drive up to Edinburgh and press refresh. As the pizza restaurant's marketing manager you need yours to be presented above your competition.

The local context of content leads us to another trend which could open up all sorts of experiential opportunities for creative marketers, driving new digital, virtual and real world experiences for the user based on their location, their preferences and their past behaviours.

Already we see augmented reality where context-appropriate content is overlaid and presented upon their view when someone looks at the world through a camera-style app. This is just the tip of the iceberg.

Virtual reality, where we can sample in advance, through our mobile device, a virtual customer journey, a tour, visit, product or service before we experience it in the real world. Again this is just a little deeper into our iceberg, but still the tip above the water.

The real value lies in the depths below the water, the deep vaults or archive content and information that we have been creating over the years. This is what we call 'big data'. Couple what we publish with our customer data and records, everything we have captured about their needs, profiles, behaviours and interests and we have at our disposal the most powerful set of insights we could dream of. It has already started because we are already listening.

Big Data and How to Enhance Customer Relationship Management

Big Data is defined by data legends IBM as "*any type of data - structured and unstructured data such as text, sensor data, audio, video, click streams, log files and more. New insights are found when analyzing these data types together.*"

So imagine. Every second of every day you and your organisation has an opportunity to capture not only slow moving customer order data but the continuous flow of comment, tweets, shares, enquiries, website mouse clicks through your site, some of which could be literally travelling at the speed of light.

The myriad of potential pieces of data you could capture multiplied by the frequency of each one, produces a tally counter that even for the smallest of businesses could spin faster than the Worldometers real time world statistics!

This is potentially HUGE, so how do you reign it in?

You ask questions first, before you look for the answers.

If you have ever looked at the relatively smaller minefield of Google Analytics you'll know that you can very quickly become swamped by information and that's not very helpful when you need to find answers. Multiply this by all of your Big Data and you get the point...

So the better approach is to decide what questions you need answered and keep those questions really tight: Be specific and keep things time-bound.

The trick with Big Data is to following the QIKI rule:

Question: Decide precisely what question you need to answer

Information: Interrogate your data with just that one question in mind and do not get distracted

Knowledge: When you find a potential answer from your data, apply your knowledge of previous experience and research to interpret what it means

Intelligence: Apply that new found interpretation to your business decisions, turning the information into intelligence for improving growth and reducing risk

Once that's done you can ask another question and repeat the process. From being tight and specific you find clarity. And remember, with the speed of Big Data available to you once you've answered a question things may have moved on and you might need to ask again! This world certainly isn't going to stop for anyone but keep questioning with the right questions and you'll find the right answers to help leverage your customer data and enhance your relationship management.

We will explore later how by understanding our customer personas and the journeys we choreograph for them we can take huge leaps forward versus our competitors as we turn the information we know into business decision-making intelligence.

Big data, and the cloud marketing that can evolve from it, can allow us to shape and personalise experiences for our customers taking into account their own preferences, opinions, needs, desires, understanding, location, calendar, privacy settings and evidence from their past behaviours. Digital marketing of tomorrow, not just the future, will be about adapting everything we do and say, in conjunction with the value our customers will demand we add. It's no longer about us, it's all about them. Winning marketers will be those who know and act on this.

How Much Data Would You Give?

People's security and loss of privacy has been a contentious issue since the start of digital data collection back in the 1990s.

As more and more private information is collected and potentially used by 'big brother', as I have so often heard an unknown community of governments, marketers and internet service providers called, I am hearing a growing population of doubters who fail to see positives in the trade-off of data giving for value received.

It's clear that the more you share about yourself in terms of location, interests, activities, preferences and purchases the more marketers can fine tune the products and services they offer to you, and how and where they offer them. The theory says the more you give, the more customised the experience you receive. Give nothing and you receive the bland, one-size-fits-all, old school, vanilla flavour. Give everything and you could receive a beautifully crafted, bespoke experience designed to satisfy your where, when, how, what and why desires, fitting perfectly into your increasingly busy lifestyle.

But the price to pay is the risk of fraudulent cloning, losing control to crime, demons inside the dark internet and perhaps some currently unknown evil force.

In this time of fast moving technological innovation it is the basic human desire for self preservation that will inevitably control the pace of adoption of the amazing opportunities in the future.

So how much data are you willing to share? There will come a point where you will need to decide. If you don't, you may get bitten anyway…

So to the internet of things (IoT), the inter-networking of physical devices, known as "connected devices" or "smart devices", buildings, and other gadgets or machines embedded with electronics, software, sensors, actuators, and an internet or network connection which enables them to collect and share data.

To the creative marketer this opens up all sorts of possibilities which takes digital marketing beyond the people-to-people and business-to-people paradigm into a brand-to-everything model.

New product development should no longer be considered in isolation from IoT potential. Any physical product may well have IoT potential to communicate 'back to base' to report faults and performance statistics, benefit from automatic upgrades to software and capability, and to interconnect with other related devices.

Marketers now have unprecedented opportunities for interacting with their products after a customer purchases them, in such a way as to listen to how they are being used, adapt future versions of products and even send added value data to them for the benefit of the device and/or the customer.

At the Retention stage of the three phases of the customer journey there is a significant opportunity to utilise IoT to enhance ongoing experience, increase engagement and think of sustained communication as more than simply social networking and an occasional email newsletter.

Think about what you could do with the products you market if you could communicate directly with and through them after your customer buys them. Do you have opportunities for cross-selling, back-selling and up-selling?

Checklist : Internet of Things

How has the Internet of Things impacted your business to date?

What opportunities do you see for your business, products or services from Internet of Things in the immediate future?

Are your competitors or others in your industry focused on the Internet of Things?

How will you keep abreast of changes and opportunities arising from Internet of Things?

What are your next steps to harnessing the Internet of Things opportunity?

2.3 PLAN : TRENDS : CREATING A COMMUNITY

One of the most significant current themes in digital communications is that of 'community'.

Online communities take many and varied forms, from special interest groups that focus on a subject, leisure pursuit or association with a brand. There are communities that focus on supporting and advocating celebrities and YouTubers and every publicly recognisable personality is likely to have a fandom community.

In business communities there are forums and groups devoted to technical aspects of innovation, new product development and specific career disciplines.

If the digital marketer can identify the communities where their target customers or partners reside, they have an opportunity to gain significant value from them.

Value from communities comes mostly in three forms: crowdsourcing; micro-tasking; and where investment is tough, crowdfunding.

Crowdsourcing is a highly useful exercise in data gathering from the community, which can by nature, be achieved at scale. Feedback about customer service, ideas for new products or perhaps market research through digital channels is scalable, cost effective and rapid.

Micro-tasking is the next level of community engagement and value where the data collected by crowdsourcing is then collated, manipulated and refined by the community. It is likely that part of the process is the undertaking of actions arising from the data.

In essence, micro-tasking is the breaking down of large actions into 'bite sized' actions, enabling the organisation to move forward quickly and effectively with implementation of ideas.

A great example of crowdsourcing and micro-tasking is Wikipedia. The community provides data at scale on every subject imaginable and then using the concept of micro-tasking, self polices that data, cleaning it, checking for accuracy and republishing where there are errors or inaccuracies.

The use of community is both engaging for the community at the same time as helping the organisation to operate at scale, at very low cost and potentially at a speed that would otherwise be impossible by using internal resources alone.

Extending the concept of community and aligning it with digital PR, the broadest and perhaps most understood of the tools in the digital marketing toolkit.

Often taken to mean 'press relations', as in press releases, it equally often is given such a wide
definition that it includes trade shows, sponsorship, investor relations and has become more Public Relations.

The UK Chartered Institute of PR defines it as "The management of reputation, the planned and sustained effort to establish and maintain goodwill and mutual understanding between an organisation and its publics".

The word 'publics' covers a very wide range of people and organisations who are interested in or affected by an organisation. These include: employees, customers, investors, regulators and suppliers.

Digital techniques have really come into their own to achieve management of communication with such diverse groups. Online PR can be said to 'leverage the network effect of the internet'. Since PR is often about people talking about people, the internet gives them many more opportunities to do so.

Generally, PR practitioners wish to maximise the number of times their organisation is mentioned in a favourable context. Digital tools such as blogs, RSS feeds, social networks offer just such opportunities.

It is vital to factor in resource and strategic pre-formed responses to such scenarios. The benefits within the social networking mix of PR are significant when positive advocacy from loyal customers makes the most noise, but there will be inherent negativity that also needs to be proactively managed as part of the process.

In practice, these characteristics manifest themselves as people having much greater choice as to where they get their information from. They can, often in a few seconds, access multiple opinions on any topic from all around the world.

They no longer have to believe what the organisation has told them e.g. through a press release. They may identify influential individuals whose opinions they listen to, for example by following them on Twitter. They may belong to special interest groups such as those on Linkedin, or take part in discussion forums such as the investors groups on Yahoo! Finance. Getting your message to stand out among this noise can be challenging to say the least. It is interesting to note that the significant majority of journalists and media source their news content from Twitter rather than the traditional press release.

There's no WE in a Social Business

The royal WE is a great way of fooling yourself that you are punching above your weight. We all do it. Or should that be, I do it.

Social business is all about personal connection and engagement. One to one communication between real people. It's not about talking to a brand or a company, it's not about selling or marketing to another organisation, it's the specific, named, real individuals inside that organisation who are our contacts.

The same works in reverse. I am often asked in marketing training sessions whether it's appropriate to represent a business online as the brand or as a distinct set of individuals who represent that brand. In almost all cases the answer must be the latter. Social business is about people not brands. It's about adding value as an individual in every interaction and not hiding behind the virtual facade of the brand or corporate firewall.

Once you begin to talk and engage using the word "I" rather than "we" you take responsibility for each and every interaction and action, your credibility and relevance rises and suddenly your importance is significantly increased to your customer engagement and to your social business itself.

Traditional PR can be enhanced and made far more efficient through digital marketing tools.

Journalist contacts can be managed efficiently through databases and emailed with only relevant
stories in far less time than previously. They can be reached through specialist tools set up to
distribute news, such as PRWeb, BusinessWire and PR Newswire as well as Twitter.

Coverage gained can be monitored through online media monitoring companies and Google Alerts can be set up.

Newsletters and e-zines (electronic magazines) can be distributed to subscribers and notifications issued to those who have requested an alert on a particular topic or event. Our comments can be posted manually or automatically on blogging sites. Our news releases will show up on Google Alerts, and all of this activity positively impacts our search engine ranking.

Social networking is used very well by journalists, professionals and celebrities too.

In the world of celebrity there is a distinct advantage in that people want to listen. Most organisations do not have that luxury so marketers and communicators, who strive to understand the needs, desires and wants of their customers, are looking at how to use social network marketing to conduct dialogue between brand and consumer.

This dialogue is essential to give marketers the opportunity to gauge opinion, satisfaction levels and desires to enable us to provide a better proposition. Social networking helps organisations achieve this as it allows marketers to seek dialogue with its customers and if an organisation is prepared to listen to the feedback, it can change its behaviours accordingly to meet their needs.

Rather than feeling dictated to, the consumer is putting more pressure on us to listen.

Writing Content for SEO

If you operate in a very busy market sector with lots of digital noise and many competitors, it's often very hard to break through with your messages using traditional marketing techniques.

Product features and benefits can be replicated by your competitors and saying you are the best, most responsive and most professional in the industry, can be instantly copied. So how do you cut through the chaos?

It's quite simple and here are some tips for establishing a foothold in those competitive search engine rankings:

1. Select the key phrases that your target audience is likely to use to search for you
2. Decide on an interesting individual with something to say who would be engaging for your audience
3. Write to them with 7-10 pertinent questions that will help to get to know them as well as add insight and thought provoking ideas
4. Publish their answers as a written interview
5. Ensure in the introduction to the interview you include all of the key phrases your target audience is likely to use to search for you
6. Publish links to the interview in all of your social networks to increase the reach
7. Monitor the outcome through your social media dashboard and for your web page through Google Analytics

It really is that simple.

A good example is the internationally popular phrase 'international sales expert' which is used by speakers, recruitment agencies and management consultants across the globe. As simple interview using this search phrase in the description and first paragraph as well as high quality insight and tips ensures Google and the other search engines view the page as high quality, current, relevant and informed... all the ingredients to appear in the top 20 of over 10,200,000 search results.

In the distant past, marketers and brand owners were in control of the way their products and services were communicated. It was a monologue.

The marketer had carte blanche over the tone, style, content and methods of communicating brand values, propositions and a product's features and benefits.

This, as we know, is no longer the case. The marketer of today, and especially the digital marketer, must take notice and account of the opinions, views and comments of others. They may arrive directly through invited means such as market research and questions posed in social media. They may also arrive uninvited where discussions begin and are conducted in discussion forums and social networks, without the input of the brand itself. They may also arrive beyond the marketer's visible horizon. In other words, some way beyond their existing networks and connections.

The latter requires the marketer to be continually sensing and listening to the wider digital environment, constantly searching for feedback and ideas, whether the sentiments are positive, neutral or negative.

The concept of participation, or two-way engagement, benefits both the brand and its consumer, and nowhere is it more useful than in consumer generated content.

Linkedin Research Example

A management consultant in a very busy market place with thousands of competing consultants needed to differentiate herself to cut through the noise.

Having carefully defined her target persona (female, senior HR professional, board member in a multinational business, busy struggling to find a work/life balance, in a male dominated sector) the consultant set out to use Linkedin to find her audience.

Whilst other consultants advertised their services, which had little or no distinction from each other, our consultant used Linkedin Groups to listen and understand the themes which her persona (let's call her Rachel), was struggling with.

Rachel's main challenge, other than needing to maintain her continuing professional development, juggle home life with work life and stand up for herself in a male dominated business world, was that she felt isolated and the only business person facing such challenges.

Rather than advertise, our consultant began interviewing Rachels and published the interviews in the online communities in which Rachel was frequently seen. Without needing to talk about *her service offering, our consultant elevated herself quickly and effectively above the competition by providing emotive and useful support and understanding.*

The resulting business enquiries were significant and sustainable, providing our consultant with great ongoing professional relationships.

In this example, Linkedin is seen not only as a publishing digital channel but also a listening one; vital subjective research, beyond the usual, well known research tools.

In the distant past, marketers and brand owners were in control of the way their products and services were communicated. It was a monologue.

The marketer had carte blanche over the tone, style, content and methods of communicating brand values, propositions and a product's features and benefits.

This, as we know, is no longer the case. The marketer of today, and especially the digital marketer, must take notice and account of the opinions, views and comments of others. They may arrive directly through invited means such as market research and questions posed in social media. They may also arrive uninvited where discussions begin and are conducted in discussion forums and social networks, without the input of the brand itself. They may also arrive beyond the marketer's visible horizon. In other words, some way beyond their existing networks and connections.

The latter requires the marketer to be continually sensing and listening to the wider digital environment, constantly searching for feedback and ideas, whether the sentiments are positive, neutral or negative.

The concept of participation, or two-way engagement, benefits both the brand and its consumer, and nowhere is it more useful than in consumer generated content.

Consumer Generated Content (sometimes called User Generated Content) CGC is the term used to describe content such as video, blogs, discussion forum posts, digital images, audio files, and other forms of media, created by consumers or end-users of an online system or service.

The vital element is that this information and content is publicly available to other consumers and for the brand to use itself, and repurpose.

Great examples of CGC include where a question is posed by a brand owner in a public online forum and the consumer community begin to add and build a story around the subject, such that the story grows a life of itself.

One of the internet's most significant CGC sites for images is flickr.com which has billions of images and over 2 million communities.

The challenge for the digital marketer seeking to take advantage of the opportunity of CGC, is to devise subjects and innovative ideas that can both stimulate sustainable user generated content at the same time as positioning their brand appropriately within or on the periphery of the discussions.

The marketer might for example, understanding the emotional needs of a target customer persona, create and offer a forum in which that persona community can engage, share and learn from others just like them. The marketer positioning themselves, in this example, as the caring facilitator. In turn this develops trust.

As a key part of a customer's journey, CGC helps them to see the brand as an integral and valuable part of a community that is relevant to them, and not just the vendor of products and services.

In highly commoditised and busy market sectors, cutting through the noise made by marketers clamouring for limited attention of the target customers, can be a thankless task.

CGC is a strategic approach that allows the marketer to position themselves as objective, relevant, current and valuable, in the eyes of the most engaged and potentially profitable customers.

Consider, as an example, an international sales agency in the highly competitive electronics industry. They have the same products to offer as the next sales agent, they have the same level of network and connections and their digital presences is quite generic and akin to their competitors. No amount of advertising or social networking will likely cut through the noise and differentiate them enough to bring them to the awareness of their target prospects and customers.

An agency like this could use CGC to create stories, discussions and innovation. They create an Experts Hub in a distinct area of their website and invite a technical guru from each of the product manufacturers they represent, to be part of a professional portal. This portal allows the technical gurus to pose questions and build discussions and build CGC, without impacting on the resources of the sales agency itself. With an objective position as the facilitator of the Experts Hub, the agency can (if agreed in advance with the invited gurus), publish many of the discussions as white papers, record audio and video interviews and panel discussions and repurpose the content in social media, enticing target prospects and customers into the portal.

As an example of a very low resource method of creating engaging, objective and highly useful content, CGC has a great part to play in the digital marketer's strategic planning as they attempt to scale their reach, cost effectively and in line with their brand evolution.

The biggest challenge is to find what will resonate best with the target audience and those supporters, or in this case, technical experts, who will support and fuel the CGC.

Initially the internet (and the websites developed for it) was a very passive medium. Companies of all sizes would create a variety of content that would then be viewed by customers. Some of these websites would incorporate some form of retail experience but mostly the customer would do little more than read and consumer.

This was often a function of the cost and complexity of creating a website, ensuring that only those companies who could afford to pay for dedicated web designers were able to generate content.

It was also limited by the mind-set of those organisations. Most of the marketing departments or media companies who developed the initial websites came from established off-line media or marketing organisations.

This passive, read-only, web had great potential, but also

created its own disadvantages such as the control of content – because only substantial organisations could afford to create and sustain any meaningful presence the majority of 'real' data was under tight editorial control.

As the number of sites tended to grow proportionately to the number of users on the internet. This control and scale initially assisted the development and acceptance of the internet.

As users became more demanding, it was expected that content would be updated on a daily or hourly basis which imposed huge costs on these companies.

Significantly, a lack of revenue from weak digital business models resulted in low levels of paying audiences and with the increase in costs businesses found the cash 'burn rate' impossible to sustain.

The customers though had experienced something of the potential of the web in engaging with companies and their favourite brands. And as they became more discerning the time was right for the arrival of web 2.0 and social media.

Virtually all the major social media sites that evolved and have since, use the method of 'tribe' and collaboration at the core of their growth plans and this ties in with the norms of off-line (real world) social interaction where the majority of individuals have a peer group of around 100-150 people (a combination of work colleagues, long term friendships from school/university and local area friendships).

These groupings interleave so that any individual's group is cross-linked into a much wider superset of groupings. Most individuals will have linkages into 3-4 groupings but some will have linkages into up to 15-20 different 'tribes' based on their demographics, work/life experience and interests.

If a social media site captures one of these inter-tribe members then, by persuading them to invite their peer group, the site can gain access to thousands of potential new members at extremely low cost. This peer group invitation is the principle reason why these sites offer to trawl email address lists for invitees.

The advocacy approach is key. Any new member of a social

media site will want to gain an active social circle rapidly to make it worthwhile being a member and investing time in the site and possibly for ego reasons. Equally the site will want them to join with other members as quickly as possible to ensure customer retention and usage, the statistics of which they can share with their potential advertisers!

Consequently social media sites always provide tools for inviting other members and customer retention is a crucial success determinant for them.

Retention (usually measured as the percentage of new users who remain with the site and active, after the first month) varies between 20% and 60% and retention rates of 40% are considered by most venture capital funders to be necessary to capture substantial market share.

Within the social media landscape it is potentially easier to identify clear segmentation for a number of reasons:

Membership – social media websites tend to be associated with 'membership' – this allows the site owner to collect and, potentially, share user demographic information. This information at its most basic level covers age, sex, and geographic location but can also include work location and company, educational level and location. A major element of the site's ability to earn revenue is to target suitable adverts to the users. This membership information is primarily the launchpad for targeting adverts as significant work is undertaken by site owners to both gauge the Click through Rate (CTR) of previous adverts and textual analysis of comments and content to select suitable adverts.

User Group Selection – members rapidly congregate into small tribes of like-minded associates. These associations can be school/work based, interest based, music focused or any of many hundreds of possible, self-created, identifiers. The difference between these associations, and tribes and the formally collected information during the membership process, is that this information is created spontaneously by the members themselves.

This makes this level of demographic information both extremely valuable to the social media sites and the marketers who wish to target them, but also extremely difficult to quantify. It is particularly valuable because the members themselves have chosen to define themselves by these relationships and groupings and so they have a real resonance with the members.

From such groups and indeed in the most active of social networks we see user generated content, which is the holy grail of social media sites. Those which can persuade the members to create the content for you rather than having to pay for its creation.

When social networking has passed a message or communication significantly beyond its normal expected 'reach' (number of people who had an opportunity to see it on their social media timeline) it could be said to have become viral.

Viral Marketing is not an entity in itself but rather an outcome when messages resonate are shared and shared again, multiple times, in a positive manner. This is in effect uber-advocacy and the ultimate goal of the digital marketer who follows best practice techniques, consistently over a long period of time.

Current, Relevant and Informed : How much should you share

I was talking to a client the other day and they asked me the profound question, "If as a service business my IP (intellectual property) is my product and you are telling me to give away ideas for free, just how much should I give away before I start to lose money because I have given away too much?"

I thought long and hard about this because it's a dilemma that all service companies who wish to become Social Businesses will face at some point after they begin to share what they do.

The dilemma is that you need to share enough of what you do to enable the prospect or client to understand what it is you offer but not too much so that they can go away and do it all by themselves. They should get enough information to make an educated decision about whether or not to engage you on their project, or at least meet for a coffee and an initial chat, but not so much that you either confuse them (because they needed you there to explain things face to face) or so that they can do it all by themselves.

So where's that all important tipping point? Well, it will vary depending on three things:

1. Your competitive position in your sector
2. The confidence you have that even if you told them how to do it they'd need you to implement it
3. Their resources to actually do what they need to do

Let me explain….

If you are well known and respected then you are likely to be able to charge more for your services and give away significantly more than a new-comer because customers will be buying you rather than just the service. This position will take time and careful planning to achieve but if you are there, then the tipping point can be quite high and you can give away lots of information for free.

Perhaps you have a unique process or system for getting the customer from A-B to achieve their goals. If you can back this up with strong case studies and testimonials then customers will likely have a stronger desire to engage you because they won't want to miss out on what their peers enjoyed and clearly if that's what it takes then they'll emotionally engage to ensure they have it for themselves.

Even if they are able to glean what they need to do themselves from the collective mass of content and ideas you share for free, it may be they don't have the internal resources of time and people to make it a reality. If this is the case then share and share away. Make them feel how great it would be to have you as part of their virtual team.

So where is your tipping point? Well think of it like a volume scale and work out the point where you would be perceived as current, relevant and informed. These three key words are just that point. From zero at the bottom of the scale where you fiercely protect your IP and don't share with anyone (how on earth do you think anyone will think you are current, relevant and informed if you do that!?) to 100% at the top of the scale where you literally give away every single thing that you do and you can watch your service business quickly go bankrupt. Somewhere on that 0-100% scale is the point at which you share the right amount of what you do, for free, through blogs, social networks and in conversation.

For me it feels at about 70%. I'm more than happy to share loads of interesting ideas and examples of others who have gone before the clients and prospects I'm speaking to. More than that and I might lose the element of surprise and the big reveal we enjoy when we take clients through our communication planning processes. Less than that and we are just another marketing business plying our services to the big wide world.

To be a Social Business perhaps we all need to move that pointer a little closer towards the top of the scale?

And of course there is the flip side of social networking publishing and 'speaking' and that is the vital ingredient of 'listening'.

Real Listening

It has been a really interesting day today in that I have experienced about one third of the incoming communication and the rest I have had to infer or make up. Let me explain.

My first experience was a positive and productive meeting with a client who's first language is not English and his command of spoken English is far from his ability to listen and understand. Add in a busy cafe with lots of ambient noise and you can imagine how hard it was initially to get the gist of the conversation.

The second was a conference call with a client who was on a speakerphone that had a mind of its own and would clip every third and fourth word when the client spoke. Add to this conversation that I was outside with background wind noise and you'll understand that this wasn't exactly a flow either.

So my average number of words clearly heard from every three or four spoken, was one. A single word which I patiently had to weave into the next one that came a second or two later.

In isolation, and as I experienced at the start of both conversations, this is way below a reasonable amount of words to allow the listener to understand what's going on and especially in a business conversation where words are long and often technical. But I found as I listened, that as I eased into the flow of the words I could hear, that soon I was able to connect with the flow and after a few minutes really dial into the intention of the speakers.

This idea of intention and flow is at the heart of really good listening. I am not claiming the highest levels of ability in the *subject but it did really make me think about how the human brain processes information and in fact how little information we really need to make good judgment and take meaning from what we experience.*

So the lessons for me today are to remember to use only words that matter and try to avoid all the waffle that we inevitably add into our monologues and the second lesson is to listen openly to everyone to ensure I get into their flow and intention. By doing so I will be demonstrating to them that I really am interested and that I really do care.

Checklist : Creating a community

What communities do you currently facilitate or are a part of?

How are your competitors building and optimising communities?

What would the ideal community look like to you and your business?

Where would your ideal community reside?

What are the next steps you will take to take the opportunities offered by the trend towards communities?

2.4 PLAN : TRENDS : AUDIO

With the aid of syndicated protocols, special software can automatically find and download the latest podcasts to a computer as soon as they become available.

Podcasts have been used distinctly as an additional medium. This element of communications has fostered competitive advantage by being used in advertising agencies as an internal communication tool.

Podcasts have significant leverage with media businesses as they have been used by radio stations, newspapers and other media channels to make their content available. The technology to do this is very cheap when compared to traditional radio and television broadcasting. This has meant that small organisations, or anybody with a website, is able to make programmes that can, and in some cases do, reach very large audiences, thereby becoming broadcasters in their own right.

It's vital the marketer of today considers this as part of their marketing planning. Not only will people be blogging and vlogging reviews of their products and services but potentially they become advocates of the company, sharing information and messages far and wide, with credibility and influence. The old press release, advertising and 'the media rules' model is long dead.

For the sake of simplicity we will take the definition of podcasting from the 2009, Arbitron / Edison Internet and Multimedia Study which defined it as: "The concept of downloading various types of longer-form online audio/video programs, in the form of digital files you can listen to at any time you choose."

Sharing a symbiotic evolution with blogging, it was started by former MTV VJ Adam Curry and blogging pioneer Dave Winer, who are credited for the rise of this medium.

Podcasts really came into prominence in 2004, when Curry, received persistent customer requests for audio-blogging so he wrote a simple programme, developed by the Open source community that automatically downloaded a podcast onto an iPod.

Despite Apple and audio-casting having a special relationship, Apple was not actively involved in the development of podcasting until mid-2005, when it joined the market on three fronts: as a source of "podcatcher", software, as publisher of a podcast directory, and as provider of tutorials on how to create podcasts with Apple products GarageBand and QuickTime Pro. Apple podcasts were always compatible with other players and programmes aside from the iPod.

Podcasts can be played on any computer or digital media portable device. This is distinct from webcasting, which implies a broadcast over the internet usually with a webcam.

The evolution of podcasting is taking a twofold approach. On one level there is a market for the professional podcast that can be made use of by organisations with brand names and their affiliation with media companies who not only offer podcasts of news updates by journalists, but also provide video news reel footage by having access to the ITN archive library.

As we know, video casting through the likes of Facebook Live and YouTube opens up a host of possibilities for using live video in the integrated communications experience.

It is within this space that marketers need to get on board, extending existing parameters and championing added value and competitive advantage through innovation.

Podcasts have two distinct advantages: they can be streamed over the internet real time; or they can be downloaded, providing the luxury of being able to be listened to as required. In order to create a podcast, more and more packages are becoming available on the market, as well as features being integrated into other aggregator systems.

Vlogs or Vodcasts are the video equivalent of the audio podcast. The release of the video enabled ipod and increased internet connections are facilitating growth of this medium and Voice Over Internet Protocol Technology (VoIP) can also be used for podcasts.

As podcasts can be listened to on various devices, they can be accessed more commonly without subscription but by direct download, which is often also included on the podcast's website.

Video podcasts are also used in multifarious ways, as stand-alones, as business communications and commonly for interviews.

The essence is free content. Marketers are now required to create and curate, as well as document, a host of content without charge. It is an investment not an instant return and therefore sometimes a challenge to justify it to management teams focused on fast return on investment of marketing resources.

Increasingly, podcasts are used as a concept of an 'enhanced medium', by educational institutions and schools, as well as used by traditional radio and TV broadcasters to re-broadcast programmes. The BBC iPlayer, introduced in July 2007 has also assisted in accelerating growth.

As media and marketing collide, more and more organisations have integrated podcasts as an add-on service. This can be used to foster brand engagement adding brand intangible value (Red Bull) and consistent attention has fostered leverage across campaigns. Public organisations such as the BBC, universities, and local authorities as well as private companies for internal communications and non-profit organisations such as The Direct Marketing Association (DMA) use it to reinforce public trust.

One of the key attractions of podcasts for advertisers is that customers on the whole are usually very well educated, having higher than average household incomes. This makes them attractive advertising targets for both online and local retailers.

Podcasting has certainly proved itself to be much more than a flash in the pan and innovative advertisers have been quick to respond.

In the UK the BMW channel which has championed integrated video and podcasts when it enlisted up-and-coming journalists to write downloadable short audio stories about a memorable car journey, whilst in the US; and Redbull have championed podcasts in America through Redbull radio and individual events. Students have made use of podcasts to prepare for their professional exams on specific topics.

Marketers are now realising how podcast advertising can work effectively within a cross-media campaign. Currently there is conflicting data as to whether podcasting as a medium is still on its ascent or if it has already peaked.

Recent years have seen the number of dedicated podcast fans up 300% driven by the speedy adoption of the likes of YouTube and Vimeo which have a low barrier to entry.

The key will be to trial, test and assess whether podcast and vodcast fits in your digital strategy.

Whilst it is fairly easy to track traffic from your website by being able to record, and analyse podcast statistics with analytics and insights.

Checklist : Audio

How do you currently use audio in your marketing communications?

Is there any best practice or good examples of the use of audio in your industry?

What tools and approaches will you take in the short term to exploit the trend in popularity of audio content?

What are you going to do today to learn more about, or harness the opportunity of audio?

3.1 PLAN : DIGITAL STRATEGY : INSIGHTS

Writing a Fast-track Digital Marketing Plan

Writing a marketing communications plan is often a chaotic and unmeasurable marketing activity for many organisations. In an attempt to help things along we recommend adopting a logical and proven strategic planning process that whilst simple in essence, delivers powerful and evidence-based continuous improvement for your organisation.

The NAPJAC format for marketing planning is a cyclical process that begins with a clear statement of the organisation's needs to ensure that everything that follows is aligned to targets rather than simply activity for activity sake.

Needs
These might be strategic goals and objectives, numbers, financial and softer targets through to short term tactical aims.

Analysis
Research and intelligence gathering about your market trends, macro situation and competitor activity will provide a clear view of the opportunities and threats that will help to shape the near term and longer term marketing that will most likely add value to the organisation.

Personas
Understanding the nuances, descriptions and unique characteristics of the real people behind your target markets will ensure you can become a social business, delivering true value and return instead of generic marketing and communication that misses the mark.

Journey
Plotting a clear customer experience from initial awareness through the building of faith and trust in the organisation at the point of conversion is as critical as the post-sale retention journey choreographed to ensure customers stay engaged and loyal for maximum lifetime value and advocacy.

Assessment
Digital dashboards for the gathering of information through the

length of the customer journey to turn into decision-enhancing intelligence that allows for continuous improvement in everything you do. Gone are the vanity metrics and in come the real measures of success against the earlier strategic goals and objectives.

Campaigns
Selection of the correct marketing tools and channels to populate the customer journeys and giving these tools job descriptions so they perform to plan is key to the most successful integrated campaigns. All tactical and day to day marketing activity can then be seen to add value to longer term goals, stripping away the unnecessary drain on resources from pointless activity.

If we want to do real and strategic digital marketing planning because we want real and sustainable results, then we need to use the the old faithful marketing mix 4Ps (Product, Price, Place, Promotion).

However in recent times this has been succeeded by the extended 7Ps marketing mix, bringing in thinking like Physical Evidence, Process and People and even that in the digital world now includes three more, bringing the total to 10Ps.

The new Ps in the mix are Planning, Prioritisation and Personalisation

Planning is a key and fundamental need for consistent reasons for being online and for integrating digital activity with traditional and offline activity.

Prioritisation is essential to understand the resource requirements for sustaining the momentum in what can be time consuming and costly activity that without a plan can appear wasteful. How will a company decide which countries and market sectors are most attractive in order to prioritise first? How will the organisation balance the short term financial objectives with longer term strategic goals? Each of these considerations needs to be carefully thought through before embarking on integrated online marketing activity.

Personalisation is also a crucial ingredient that we had not seen before digital, and where the 'one size fits all' model of marketing falls down. In the online world, consumers and business people alike are seeking a customised, almost bespoke level of service and engagement and the most successful online brands are providing such personalisation in their customer journey to inspire long term loyalty and optimum lifetime value.

People is still a key P in the marketing mix. Organisations must consider if they have the experience internally to plan and delivery digital and social networking activity. If not then some integration of third party specialists and agencies may be required for the initial research, auditing and planning as well as the ongoing delivery of campaigns and supporting tactical activity.

This leads to the consideration of Place where in an online space organisations operate on a 24/7 365 days a year basis. Online never sleeps and it is vital that the processes, systems and any required automation, deliver an integrated customer experience irrespective of time of day and day of the week. This becomes particularly important when considering that not all working weeks are Monday to Friday 9-5. In Gulf States for example the traditional working week is Sunday to Thursday. It goes without saying that organisations in the Far East are operating on very different physical time zones to those in the Far West.

The online experience never sleeps, and as such, organisations must prepare to deliver a consistent offer, irrespective of from where in the world the visitor or customer is making contact.

This leads to a consideration of the back office systems and processes in a language and on terms appropriate to the customer. If, as is the case with most organisations, English is the predominant first online language, it is strategically important to consider how this might impact the customer experience if a priority target country or region does not have English, or the English alphabet as a regularly used and acceptable language.

The choice of third party websites and social networking platforms is also an important consideration. The assumption of the dominance of Facebook, Twitter, and LinkedIn, may or may not be applicable to some target countries where locally popular social networks are significant. Examples of this can be seen in Italy, China, India and Brazil.

When planning to serve more than your local area or region, the consideration of provision of customer service is very important. Lack of physical presence in a particular place means a greater reliance on third party support and delivery services, and an extension of the traditional supply chain as well as after-sales service. In this instance the careful selection of online messages and levels of promise must be in line with the digital promises and marketing to ensure the customer perceives the value of the promise in line with the actual experience received.

The broader the range of regions and countries served online, the potentially wider the range of marketing, products and services required. The assumption that new regions will accept the existing way of marketing and doing business may not provide enough value.

Local product and service variants as well as website styles and tuning of digital marketing activity may be necessary.

Pricing can also be a sensitive issue across international borders and the complexity of online legislation, regulations and local tax implications all affects how organisations can do business.

The Steps to your Digital Marketing Plan

Sports coaches tell their proteges to focus. You listen to the radio and you tune in. When you take a photograph you focus the lens. Everywhere you look there are examples of focusing.

To focus is to set the centre of interest or activity. Synonyms include, focal point, central point, centre of attention, hub, heart, core. The dictionary definition includes "the state or quality of having or producing clear visual definition". A focus is sharp, crisp, distinct, clear, well defined, well focused and a device on a lens that can be adjusted to produce a clear image.

A verb I particularly like is to "adapt to the prevailing level of light and become able to see clearly".

When you are creating a strategy, that all important route map to a better, stronger and more robust future, what better than to think about the verb 'focus'.

By focusing you strip away all of the unnecessary, all of the distractions, all of those things that can encourage you to stray from your path.

If you are doing things today, right now, that are not adding direct value to the achievement of those goals that you set in your strategy then you are doing things that are moving you away from it. Focus is the answer.

Take a look at everything you have done so far today. Which things have been focused on your strategy and which things have been distractions? **Make** *a pact with yourself and your ToDo list that you will only focus on tasks, actions and steps that move you ever closer to achieving your goals. Everything else is a distraction and once you recognise each thing then you can decide not to do it again.*

Careful task and action planning and focusing on the clear steps to your goals is at the heart of successful strategic planning and delivery.

To create sustainable, profitable growth requires a coordinated, prioritised and realistic strategic business development plan.

Real business development comes as a result of combining marketing strategy and tactics with the closure of sales opportunities through appropriate channels.

Business development happens through using carefully chosen planning techniques and balancing smart goals and targets with considered, commercial realism.

To begin, it's vital to work systematically through a 10 step marketing process to create the environment from which profitable sales opportunities can be secured.

This approach allows for launch, consolidation and growth of new business in selected marketplaces and regions.

Effective marketing planning, the essential first step in creating a profitable sales funnel, is a four stage process that takes companies seeking growth through ten stages from research and planning to delivery, the results and incremental profit from which will help to ensure a long term future for their products.

The Research stage includes local market audits, competitor analysis, scaling of market size and prioritisation of opportunities against the capabilities and resources of the business.

The Planning stage creates smart, strategic objectives and a marketing strategy as well as plotting customer journeys to ensure the sales and marketing experience is optimised for distributors, partners and customers alike. Identification of the Unique Selling Proposition as this stage is key and sets the business apart from the noise of the competition, thereby warming up the potential for lead generation in preparation for complimentary sales activities.

The Delivery stage looks after the launch and ongoing tactical marketing to support sales growth in selected territories. Crucial to this activity is the creation and roll-out of an engaging content strategy which will potentially also open up opportunities for further product introductions into chosen distribution channels in the future. The most effective sales and marketing activities now focus on delivering positive customer outcomes rather than simply the features and benefits of products. Understanding and communicating how the products add real value to the customers' world, is at the heart of successful business development.

The Reporting stage is all about results and these take the form of a business development dashboard to ensure continuous and ongoing improvement is made to the marketing and distribution plans to maximise profit for, and return on investment across the product portfolio.

Extending the marketing mix further in a digital content the marketer must also now consider planning, which as we have seen, is a key and fundamental need for consistent reasons for being online and for integrating digital activity with traditional and offline activity.

Organisations must consider if they have the experience internally to plan and delivery digital and social networking activity. If not then some integration of third party specialists and agencies may be required for the initial research, auditing and planning as well as the ongoing delivery of campaigns and supporting tactical activity.

It is essential to understand the resource requirements for sustaining the momentum in what can be time consuming and costly activity that without a plan can appear wasteful.

How will a company decide which countries and market sectors are most attractive in order to prioritise first? How will the organisation balance the short term financial objectives with longer term strategic goals? Each of these considerations needs to be carefully thought through before embarking on integrated online marketing activity.

A crucial, more recent, ingredient that we had not seen before digital is true personalisation. Personalisation is where the 'one size fits all' model of marketing is finally removed.

In the online world, consumers and business people alike are seeking a customised, almost bespoke level of service and engagement and the most successful online brands are providing such personalisation in their customer journey to inspire long term loyalty and optimum lifetime value.

The online experience never sleeps, and as such, organisations must prepare to deliver a consistent offer, irrespective of from where in the world the visitor or customer is making contact.

This leads to a consideration of the back office systems and processes in a language and on terms appropriate to the customer. If, as is the case with most organisations, English is the predominant first online language, it is strategically important to consider how this might impact the customer experience if a priority target country or region does not have English, or the English alphabet as a regularly used and acceptable language.

In selecting the best tactical mix and when formulating the step by step campaign journey, we need to carefully consider the target audience, messages, communications tools and our resources requirements and as such we are now ready to construct our integrated digital communications mix.

Checklist : Insights

What are your opportunities for using media, channels and content types that you aren't currently optimising?

What are your perceived threats to your marketing, position, brand or business? Often these threats come from competitors, trends and capabilities of other people and organisations.

Have you completed a forensic analysis of your competitors' digital marketing activities? Look at their website, social networks, engagement with customers, style, tone and effectiveness of digital content, their tactical campaigns and their longer term strategic intent. Note if they focus on specific themes, products and services.

Which trends are going to affect you in the coming months and years? Things like your customers' mobility, use of smart mobile devices, the internet of things, specific changes and trends in your industry. Some trends will be macro (big things you cannot affect like the political environment, financial markets, etc.) and some will be micro trends (more local things such as your supply chain, new brands entering your marketplace, behaviours of specific customers you'd like to target.

3.2 PLAN : DIGITAL STRATEGY : SMART KPI, OBJECTIVES, STRATEGY

Too many companies jump straight into digital marketing and especially into social media with little understanding of what is required in order to do the job well and vitally, without understanding the true reasons why digital marketing is important to them in the first place.

Many establish presences on social media platforms with little thought to the commitment needed
to do a credible job. Many executives have seen this as a peripheral activity, establish a presence and then fail to maintain an up to date site or use the media to its fullest extent. This is equivalent to placing a magazine advert but failing to give the correct company address or phone number for enquiries.

Rather than spreading resources too thinly and consequently having a negative impact on the reputation of your brand, it is important to carry out a digital marketing audit.

There are a number of fundamental building blocks when you are assessing your current situation in digital marketing. Once you establish this baseline and importantly what the business or organisation goals are, in the short, medium and longer term, you will be in a far stronger position to both monitor improvement and also report back how your digital activity is helping to deliver strategic objectives.

Weaving together the audit gives you the base from which to build a relevant, engaging, profitable and sustainable digital marketing strategy:

Step 1 - Organisation drivers
- What are the digital strengths and weaknesses of your organisation, versus your competitors?
- Have you assessed previous campaigns and digital activities?
- What are your organisation objectives from which to build your digital targets?
- What Key Performance Indicators (KPIs) does your organisation use to monitor performance?
- What does success look like to your organisation?

Which Unique Selling Propositions (USPs) can you communicate that can't currently be copied by your competitors

Do you have any upcoming events, product or service launches, changes or announcements that you could use in your digital marketing content?

- What offline marketing needs to be integrated with your digital?
- Who are the key stakeholders for your digital plan, both internal and external?

How do you manage reputation and reduce risk?

Step 2 - Your people
- What available staff resources do you have at your disposal and how much available time do they have?
- Is there appropriate knowledge and experience in the team or will you need to outsource?
- Do your online promises and marketing match your actual delivery?

What internal cost constraints do you have?

Can you identify others outside of the marketing function who could contribute, perhaps as 'faces of the organisation'?

Step 3 - Your technology
- What database and customer relationship management (CRM) systems are in place and are they
appropriate?
- Do you have appropriate privacy and data protection protocols and processes?
- Which digital tools are already in use and what insights are coming from them that you are acting on?
- Do you have a digital dashboard collecting and reporting along the length of your customers' journey?

Step 4 - The bigger picture
- What competitor activity both online and offline could impact your planning and delivery?
- Do you know what partner and supplier activity works well and what might be piggybacked upon?
- Have you analysed your competitors to establish opportunities and potential threats from their current and upcoming activities
- What trends and future expectations of your marketplace are appropriate to factor in?
- What are the most appropriate digital tools available within your planning timeframe?

- Have you considered the impact of Politics, Environment, Social, Technological, Economic and Legislation (such as GDPR)?
- Prioritise customer or market segments to identify the reachable and most engaged customer groups
- Who are the key influencers in each market segment you wish to target? This could be associations, media, customers, bloggers, vloggers.
- Do different cultures, locations and languages across customer segments need different sub-plans? Is there an international flavour of your target audience requiring translation or specialist treatment?
- What are the key market and customer trends in behaviour, acceptance and expectations?

Addressing each of these in an initial digital marketing audit allows you to set up appropriate and relevant baselines from which to build strategic and tactical plans to achieve your online goals.

Using these criteria above you would now be in a position to construct a digital SWOT Analysis to strike a balanced view of the strengths, weaknesses, opportunities and threats you will take into your digital planning.

An effective way of presenting the SWOT Analysis is generally a 2x2 matrix. Your plans can then consider how your digital activities will support turning threats into opportunities, and weaknesses into strengths.

Know Your Competitors

"If you know the enemy and know yourself, you need not fear the result of a hundred battles. If you know yourself but not the enemy, for every victory gained you will also suffer a defeat. If you know neither the enemy nor yourself, you will succumb in every battle." Sun Tzu : The Art of War.

As a key starting point in any marketing planning activity and then the subsequent delivery of marketing communications and business development, we need to establish at the outset, the competitive position of the business. It is not possible to fully succeed in business without a clear understanding of the alternatives that your customer is considering.

A great starting point is to remain humble and consider that you have, and are, nothing particularly special. From there, you and your organisation can build a hunger and desire, that matched with competitive acumen, will keep you at least one step ahead in your competitive positioning.

By competitive position, what we mean is the position in the marketplace that the business takes versus other companies offering similar products and services. It's vital to think about this from a market-by-market basis as there may be different competitors operating in different markets.

Taking the charity sector as an example, a Competitor Review would establish the direct competition in this sector for equivalent services offered by other charities. Many of these will be very obvious with alternative charities offering similar and equivalent donor benefits and propositions.

There will be a Market Leader (number 1 in the marketplace), Market Challenger (number 2, vying for the top spot), Market Followers (a larger number of organisations who watch, follow and copy the big 2), Market Nichers (potentially profitable organisations who focus on a niche offer in the same marketplace).

When the relative competitive position is known, the organisation can strategically decide who to monitor, who to emulate, the trends to watch, things to avoid. It is vital to review and respond to campaign activities of the key, direct competitors.

Interestingly in the case of charities, where there is a limit to the available purse (the total amount that the market place of donors is willing to donate to that sector), the 'share of purse' spread across the competitors, is a key measure that points to their relative positions. In your sector, what's YOUR market share? Consider both the volume of sales in your sector and the value of sales, when answering the question. If this question is too hard to answer then there is work to be done in reviewing more deeply, who you are up against.

It is not possible to create a SWOT analysis for an organisation before conducting a competitor review like this, because strengths are only strengths when compared to another organisation.

Opportunities may come not only from macro trends but also from tactical things that competitors are or are not doing. Threats will be identifiable as they appear and weaknesses can be addressed by a coordinated action plan.

In some instances a competitor review may need to consider indirect competitors. In other words, other companies not offering similar products and services but delivering customers needs by other, unrelated methods. There is always a 'customer does it themselves' option and as such this could also be an indirect competitor.

As Sun Tzu said, "To Know Your Enemy, You Must Become Your Enemy". Your work in competitive auditing is never done. For every move you make, your competitor will make a counter move, and if they don't, then you should be even more afraid.

Checklist : Smart KPIs, objectives, strategy, action plans and measures

What are your (smart) higher level business goals, for which your digital marketing will add value and help you to achieve?

Think about the resources available to you; The available people, budget and time?

What are your strengths and weaknesses versus your competition and alternative products and services available to your target audience?

What are your smart KPIs, based on your resources and business goals?

Have you stated your business goals both in the immediate and short term as well as those supporting your longer term vision. It's essential that all digital marketing activity and content publishing in some way supports these goals. Measurement of success is only possible when you are clear and smart (specific, measurable, achievable, realistic and time-bound) about your goals.

Can you ensure your business goals balance both objective (numbers and financials) with subjective (softer aims, such as customer satisfaction and brand awareness)?

What is your strategic aim; the position in which you are aiming to be in 3 -5 years time?

How will your strategic aim look and feel?

How will your customers perceive you when you have reached your strategic aim?

Have you split your strategic aim into end of year tactical aims for each of the years in your planning timeframe?

Taking the first of your tactical aims (year one) what are your month by month action plans to help achieve your aims?

3.3 PLAN : DIGITAL STRATEGY : INTERNAL COMMUNICATIONS

Planning a digital marketing campaign is not dissimilar for the most part from planning any other marketing campaign. The internet and associated technologies have simply added more tools to the marketing mix.

FLOSS : 5 Tips For Business Growth Through Digital Marketing : Finance, Leadership, Operations, Strategy and Sales (FLOSS)

Not a word there about social media, brochures, direct mail campaigns and advertising. The most value you are likely to get from your marketing is when you properly utilise the full definition of the function.

Contrary to popular belief, marketing is not only about communications and promotions. How the term has been used and abused over the years by low value tactical players. Ask anyone on the street what they understand by the word marketing and the answer will almost certainly contain a variety of promotional terms.

True marketing is a strategic science. It should consider creating and supporting the following 5 elements of successful business management:

Finance - work closely, hand in hand with the accountants and forecasters. Who better than marketing to add in some customer and market focused reality to the spreadsheets.

Leadership - so often in lowly positions, elevate your best marketers into leadership roles and all them to drive the voice of the customer throughout the organisation.

Operations - align your marketers with the engine house of the business to help plan production volumes and product specifics. If marketing leads the delivery of the customer journey you'll see great value returned.

Strategy - marketing has so many invaluable tools to help drive the business forward towards a common goal. Let the marketers plan, delivery, monitor, analyse and report and you'll see so much more than how they colour in the pictures and join the dots in the company brochure.

Sales - it really is possible to align your sales and marketing for mutual benefit. It all starts with common goals and shared incentives.

Think today about how you can redefine marketing in your own business and push for more value and evidence of return on investments.

We need to start by setting objectives.

1. Target Audience; this is a critical starting point is to define exactly who you are talking to. Who is your key audience in the campaign and which other customer segments might benefit from hearing your messages too?

2. Objectives; you cannot run an effective campaign without establishing your targets at the outset. What are your strategic targets, the ones that will help you to deliver your bigger organisational goals? What key performance indicators are you going to use so you can monitor how the campaign is progressing and check the success at the end?

3. Messages; what is the lead message or proposition for this campaign? What back up messages will support the lead message? Are these consistent with other campaigns you have run or are running and consistent with your brand?

4. Creative; what electronic and printed materials do you need for your campaign? Have you factored the cost of producing and delivering these into your campaign plan? The costs of these need to be included in your objectives because if you over spend the profitability of your campaign will reduce.

5. Channels; how will your target audience experience your campaign? Where will they see, hear and sample it? Think both traditional channels like PR, advertising and direct mail as well as electronic channels such as web, email and social media. Join all your delivery channels together in a nice simple visual so everyone knows where your campaign is happening and what is expected as an outcome from each element.

6. Customer Journey; setting a choreographed, step by step journey through the three phases of engagement to create Awareness, Conversion of that awareness into a customer and then Retention of the customer to stimulate loyalty and potentially advocacy with their peers. The journey is literally a step by step, click by click, route map of links and content and tools.

7. Timing; everything at each step needs to be time bound so set some realistic yet challenging timescales for each element. Identify your start date and target end date but remember to build in a review stage so you can analyse and learn from the outcomes and results of your campaign.

A well proven model for structuring your digital marketing plan beyond the objective setting is PR Smith's SOSTAC® Planning System (Smith, 2011). SOSTAC® is a registered trademark of PR Smith, www.prsmith.org. This stands for: Situation Objectives Strategy Tactics Actions Control

This model highlights that once you have populated each of the above it's vital to set clear key performance indicators (KPIs) which will provide evidence of what is working and what needs to be improved.

Digital Marketing Project Management

Digital Marketing Project Management, be it a campaign, new product development or the creation of a new website, requires careful management of people, process and time and it is always best to build it from the ground up rather than just jumping straight in.

Step One: Marketing Audit
Engage everyone in the organisation to feed in information and knowledge. Gather customer and competitor information and look for trends. Have you tried this before? If you have then look at what happened before. If this is your first time with a project of this kind then search on the web to find similar experiences.

Step Two: Marketing Information System
Collate and aggregate the information in a central management or marketing information system that will help you to create

intelligence from the audit. Bounce the intelligence off others in the organisation to sanity check it and make sure it's relevant, current and appropriate. Embrace any changes that this intelligence suggests. This stage is key for a learning organisation seeking to make step changes in how it operates.

Step Three: Business Case

Don't shirk the full business case. Follow the logic and test all assumptions, desires and goals. Make sure everything you are going to invest in (people, products, processes) will all benefit from a return on your investment of energy and budget. Test things until you think they are watertight. If you can't stand up in front of everyone in the organisation from your colleagues to the CEO and be confident in your story, then you still have work to do.

Step Four: Risk Analysis

The best organisations who invest in people have a blame-free culture. Open up all the risks that your project faces and look them directly in the eye. Do some scenario planning. What if? Rate each risk for likelihood of happening and for impact if it does happen. Rate both scales 1-10. Multiply the two numbers and you'll get a league table for risk management and mitigation. There is no better way of testing out your business case and inspiring confidence across your organisation than having a clear risk mitigation plan.

Step Five: Project Plan

This is where most people have already jumped in and they have missed out on the four crucial earlier steps. In your plan set a critical path, the minimum set of key milestones you must have achieved to take your project from inception to completion. What tools will you need to run and communicate your project? Is your project driven predominantly by time, by budget or by resources? You need to know because that's how it'll be rated by others. Inspire non-frantic urgency throughout your project team and remember the golden words of marketing project management, collaboration and communication. You are responsible for coordinating thoughts, feelings and behaviours, as well as tasks.

Step Six: Management and Reporting

Keep a learning log so you have a record to keep as a project legacy. Always think of process evolution because your project and the people in it will be very different by the end of it all. Remember the outcomes. What was it you committed to delivering in your business case? Do you stand by those goals? Did you deliver return on investment? It should always be a 360 degree review. Take feedback on the chin, both good and bad. Use Balanced Scorecard to ensure you report and share not only task completion but some of the softer but equally vital people-centric outcomes.

And when you look back at your marketing project ask yourself two questions, "Strategically, did I really deliver a return on investment?" and "Am I a better person for the experience?". I hope you can answer yes to both.

Checklist : Internal communications

With your digital strategy in mind, who will you need to communicate your plans with and how?

Are there any others who will assist you in delivery of your digital strategy and if so what are their roles and how will you brief them?

What is your current preferred medium for internal communications in your business, including reporting and news updates?

How can you improve your internal communications with all stakeholders?

Have you created and are using a consistent process for internal communications to ensure timeliness and relevance for all involved?

What will you improve today in your internal communications?

3.4 PLAN : DIGITAL STRATEGY : RETURN ON INVESTMENT

When you consider planning and integration, where are you now and where do you want to be?

Fundamental questions like this are at the heart of great planning and the first consideration is your relative position in your marketplace.

Five Forces is a well established and proven model that considers the balance of power between different organisations in a market sector, and helps to present the attractiveness and potential profitability of the sector.

This is a strategic tool that provides a broad overview of the relative strength of taking a particular market position

Force 1: Threat of New Entry
Force 2: Buyer Power
Force 3: Threat of Substitution
Force 4: Supplier Power
Force 5: Competitive Rivalry

If a start-up can operate in a sector without investment - then it is likely to be a threat.

SmartInsights.com suggests asking yourself the questions:
What's the threat of new businesses starting in this sector?
How easy is it to start up in this business?
What are the rules and regulations?
What finance would be needed to start-up?
Are there barriers to entry which give you greater power?
Buyer Power
Where there are fewer buyers, they often control the market. Questions here include:
How powerful are the buyers?
How many are there?
Can the buyers get costs down?
Do they have the power to dictate terms?
Threat of Substitution

If there are available alternatives then the threat of substitution increases.

How easy is it to find an alternative to this product or service?

Can it be outsourced? Or automated?

Supplier Power

Markets where there are few suppliers means the suppliers retain the power

Examine how many suppliers are in the market?
Are there a few who control prices?
Or many so prices are lower?
Do your suppliers hold the power?
How easy is it to switch, what's the cost?

Competitive Rivalry

Markets where there are few competitors are attractive but can be short-lived. These are highly competitive markets with many companies chasing the same work reduce your power in the market.

What's the level of competition in this sector?

What's the competitor situation? Many competitors and you're all in a commodity situation or a few?

Smart-Insights provides some examples of how Porter's five Forces can be applied to a business, especially one that is looking to enter a new market or is considering it's relative market position and how the sector(s) in which it operates is evolving.

1. Threat of New Entrants

An example is web design, as there are independents in every location. This is an easy market to enter with few requirements, other than skills, initiative and relevant hardware and software. This does mean there are many new entrants!

2. Buyer Power

An example is the grocery sector since supermarkets tend to retain power over suppliers due to volume and price of contracts. They dictate terms, set prices and can possibly end agreements at any time.

3. Threat of Substitution

The substitute to all services is DIY. For example hairdressing or writing a will. Focus is on expertise, customer service or added value.

4. Supplier power

Some sectors have monopolistic (one) or oligopolistic (few)

suppliers, such as utility companies. Sometimes customers have little choice i.e. where to buy domestic water suppliers though this is changing.
In the jewellery sector, diamond suppliers often hold the power and can set prices, withhold supply and restrict sales.

5. Competitive rivalry

These include Estate agents, web design and office stationary. Many competitors often buy on price.

Creating Flow in Digital Marketing Communications

I am going to take a few analogies to set the scene about how important it is to create and maintain flow in your marketing communications.

In rivers, dams are an inhibitor that prevents the energy of the river flowing and benefitting everyone and everything downstream. In your house or office you have many lights and lamps but without the energy of the electricity flow there is no illumination and you sit in the dark. In projects when there are bottlenecks; times when there is not enough resource or perhaps limited experience or knowledge; the flow of the activities and actions stalls. In finance we always talk about cashflow, the love hate relationship between invoicing in a timely manner and getting paid on time to enable the fulfilment of debt commitments.

In spirituality there are many who believe the intentions you set in your life work with the flow of the energy in the universe and conspire to deliver to you everything in your vision. And with friendships they only work well when there's a regular two-way flow of love, value and caring; in all ways the flow of human energy.

So with these examples in mind and an understanding that flow is all around us and an integral part of how the world works we come to using this in developing more effective marketing communications.

The rule is simple and we see it in numerous situations. It's called Drip Feed.

By maintaining regular, low level but useful engagement in all your marketing communications you remain front of mind for your target audience. Gone are the monthly newsletters where you would have waited for a month to relay that golden nugget of information and by the time the audience receives it then it's out of date. Gone is the 'I leave my social networking until Friday afternoon because it fits my calendar' as that is simply a burst of meaningless energy and likely to arrive when your target audience is away and focused on other things. Gone is the paid advertising of old where you had to invest your hard earned cash on the off chance that your audience would see your advertisement and even less likely that they would respond.

The best way to create flow in your marketing communications is undoubtedly to think of drip feeding your messages. Balance them by the Rule of Thirds and ensure that little and often, and at the times you've researched that your audience is most likely to engage, is the way you communicate. In this way you ensure that there is a steady and positive flow of incoming engagement for your organisation.

Building Blocks of the Digital Marketing Audit

There are five fundamental building blocks when you are assessing your current situation in digital marketing.

Weaving together the audit of these five elements gives you the platform from which to build a relevant, engaging, profitable and sustainable digital marketing strategy:

Organisation Drivers
Strengths, weaknesses, opportunities and threats inside and around your organisation
Assessment of what's gone before, what worked and what didn't
Organisation objectives and targets, from which to build your digital targets
Resources available, including budget, people and time
Your Key Performance Indicators (KPIs) and what does success look like to your organisation
Unique Selling Propositions (USPs)
What traditional and offline marketing and communication needs to be integrated with digital
Who are the key stakeholders, sponsors and management for your digital plan
How do you manage reputation and reduce risk

Your People
What staff resource do you have at your disposal

Is there appropriate knowledge and experience in the team or will you need to outsource

What is already in place and working today

Do your online promises and marketing match your actual delivery of product and service

Establish internal cost constraints

Your Technology
What database and customer relationship management systems are in place and are they appropriate

Do you have appropriate privacy and data protection protocols and processes

Which digital tools are already in use and what insights and analytics are coming from them

Do you have a digital dashboard collecting and reporting along the length of the customer journey

World Around You
What competitor activity both online and offline will impact your planning and delivery

Do you know what partner and supplier activity works and what might be piggybacked

Competitor gap analysis can establish opportunities and potential threats

Does your digital planning encompass the entire supply or value chain

What trends and future expectations of the competitor environment are appropriate to factor in

The Big Picture
What are the most appropriate digital tools within your planning timeframe

Have you considered the impact of Politics, Environment, Social, Technological, Legislation, Economic factors

Prioritisation of customer or market segments to identify the reachable and most engaged customer groups

Who are the key influencers in each market segment. This could be associations, media or customers

Do different cultures, locations and languages across customer segments need different sub-plans

What are the key market and customer trends in behaviour, acceptance and expectations

Answering each of these questions in an initial digital marketing audit allows you to set up appropriate and relevant baselines from which to build strategic and tactical plans to achieve your online goals.

As we have already discussed, key to the essence of effective digital marketing is planning.

Without a plan to glue together potentially disparate activities and thinking there is a real challenge to measure effectiveness and outcomes which in themselves are the required return on investment of time, resource and budget.

A good digital marketing plan should be integrated with broader marketing plans and further upstream, to corporate strategy, plans and business objectives.

An effective plan ensures the organisation measures the right things to grow the business through online marketing and continuously improves to provide the highest level of relevant products, services, messages and conversations with prospects and customers across the world.

It is vital to think about digital marketing as a balance between short term and long term, tactical and strategic. But even with the short term it may not be as effective in directly generating sales in a commercial environment as the rest of the organisation might like to believe.

Setting reasonable expectations about what each digital marketing tool will deliver is a key element in setting the boundaries and prioritising the most effective way forward.

As an example, LinkedIn is one of the most popular business social networking tools but can you really sell through it? You see a huge community of business professionals, many of whom could be ripe for picking when it comes to selling your products and services. They are there in front of you just a few keyboard presses away. You do not have to call them, meet them or break through a gatekeeper, receptionist or PA. Surely then this is the easiest and most effective sales tool available?

One of the key mistakes that people make when trying to overtly self-promote or increase the profile of their business or brand is to jump straight in and use the power of research and targeting to send unsolicited sales messages to communities, groups and individuals. This is not what LinkedIn was designed for, and the same is true for other social media in the digital marketing mix. It is much more a collaborative and networking community; a platform for sharing of ideas, thoughts and opinions. Something like a business networking breakfast on steroids and all from the comfort of your desk or sofa. But therein lies a potential frustration. Just how much can you and should you overtly 'sell' on a business social networking platform.

TTF Model for Digital Marketing Prioritisation : Today, Tomorrow, Future

Not everything has the same value. Some things have a value today (cashflow, survival, etc.).

Some things have a value tomorrow (growth, security, etc.). The most important things have a value in the future (vision, destiny).

Make sure you carefully prioritise every project, customer and task using the TTF Model so that you can think about them on relative and appropriate terms. The best way to maintain a great balance is to do just that; Balance some to give value today, some tomorrow and vitally, remember the most important ones are guiding you to your future.

The general principle is to not think of or use the words 'sell' or 'sales' when you are thinking about LinkedIn or social media. Giving reasons to buy, yes. Adding value, yes.

It may be part of your digital hub and it may create enquiries and leads that could be an eventual outcome and many are generating excellent high quality business leads from it. But it is far better and safer to use and think strategically about words like 'influence', 'sharing', 'intelligence', 'collaboration'. These are words much more akin to the attitudes and thought patterns of others when they are using LinkedIn. That is the mindset they are in when they are there, so it is best to communicate with them at that time on their terms and in a style appropriate to how they are feeling:

- Research – find groups of like-minded individuals, focused around your interests, products and market sector
- Listen – listen to the discussion threads, comments and the atmosphere inside debates that interest you
- Contribute – add value to the debate, comment positively and sometimes critically, stimulate others to comment back
- Lead – start new discussions, pose interesting new angles to old stories
- Give – provide links to resources, videos, training, tutorials and informative blogs. Share and share alike

Build your credibility, your value and your presence before beginning to ask for leads, new business or overtly promote your cause. Build a following and professional standing on LinkedIn before you even consider the word 'sales' and you will be surprised just how receptive others will be to what you say in the future.

How to Use Gap Analysis in your Digital Marketing Planning

There's a school of thought that talks about setting intention and then trusting the universe that everything will manifest when it's ready. There is also an ideology in most cultures that those who choose to work hardest will receive the largest rewards. This has more recently become those who also work smartest.

A great example comes from sport and Team Sky, the world beating cycling team whose riders have won Tour de France and almost every other major road cycling event.

The team's top riders are known to not only start training a little earlier than the others and finish a few kilometres later but also to obsessively monitor every element of their lives whilst awake and asleep. This obsession with detail takes things down to fractions of a percentage in improvements to a multitude of things, from sleep patterns, diet, travel arrangements, training plans, leisure time, psychology and more.

Like many business sectors, where margins are so tight, incremental improvements in every facet of the situation, by just 1% each, can accumulatively result in significant gains. What might go unnoticed by others because of the almost miniscule significance of an individual element, can have a profound effect *on the combined performance.*

With this in mind, think about your own organisation. Break down your organisation into segments such as product, promotion, people, operations, sales, leadership, management, pricing, purchasing, remuneration, performance monitoring, reporting, innovation, profitability ... you will have many other areas to consider.

Imagine making 1% improvements to each of the 14 elements outlined above... collectively what would that mean for you and your business? How about assigning the challenge of 1% improvements to each colleague.... balanced scorecard is a great tool for helping them to report back. Then take the combined improvements score and let us all know how this helped you drive your business forward.

Strategy is only as effective as the tactics it stimulates. Tactics are only as good as the action plans that evolve from them. Actions plans only work when the content that fuels them drives the right target customer personas through the right journey to reach defined targets, resulting in pre-defined behaviour and sales.

Bringing all of these threads together in the digital marketer's activities is the development of a cohesive and well-defined marketing campaign. The purpose of a digital marketing campaign is to encourage and facilitate a pre-defined behaviour.

This behaviour is likely to be defined in the Conversion point of the customers' journey. It might be a product or service sale, the signing of a contract, or another pre-defined action whereby a prospect converts into a customer.

The campaign, even though it may be defined as a digital marketing campaign, is likely to also have a blend of offline tools and moments where the target customer experiences things in the real world as well as through their screen.

As we have already established, the customer journey, and in this instance the campaign, must consider every step of engagement from the very first time they encounter the start of the campaign, through to and ongoing retention and continued engagement post-purchase.

The RACE Framework of Reach, Act, Convert, Engage is a very useful checklist to begin the construction of the campaign flow.

Reach - establish which social networks and publishing tools you will need to include in your campaign to draw the target customer into the content hub. The target customer is exploring and considering their options.

Act - decide the hub (possibly within your website) where you will direct your target customers their journey. The customer is making their decision at this point.

Convert - the conversion point, likely to be the point of purchase, is where the customer needs to have established trust in your brand and what they are purchasing. The extended digital marketing mix will come into play at this point in their journey.

Engage - post-purchase, where the prospect has now become a customer, is when and through which digital marketing tools, to help stimulate advocacy (sharing of their great experience with their peers, colleagues, family and friends).

Checklist : Return on investment (ROI)

Rate either strong or weak: your current website, each social media account, your blog, your vlog, the consistency of your brand messages, tone of voice and style and the impact and engagement you have on your target customers?

How do you and your business measure ROI?

Knowing how much resource you are committing to your current digital marketing activities, what will you change to improve ROI for your business?

4.1 OPTIMISE : PERSONAS : DEFINE, FIND AND LISTEN

Economic Times defines segmentation as a "means to divide the marketplace into parts, or segments, which are definable, accessible, actionable, and profitable and have a growth potential. In other words, a company would find it impossible to target the entire market, because of time, cost and effort restrictions. It needs to have a 'definable' segment - a mass of people who can be identified and targeted with reasonable effort, cost and time."

In digital marketing we take this to the next level of detail by creating highly focused 'customer personas' taking into consideration not only demographics, socio-economic data and behaviour but descriptions of lifestyle, preferences, digital usage and more.

The concept of using personas in your digital marketing is all about creating a deep understanding of exactly who you are targeting with your digital content and the journey you are taking them through from the first time they ever encounter you, to the point they become a loyal advocate.

This is about filtering. Whilst it may feel attractive to consider your target audience as 'everyone' it's always the case that by filtering out the masses and focusing on the most valuable, profitable (or however you define success) customer, your digital efforts will be much more effective. It pays to be very specific. Avoid generalisations and make things really precise. Their age should be 34 for example, rather than 'between' 25 and 45.

Think of this process as about creating quality more than quantity. Once you have established quality you can scale up and attract the quantity of these same personas.

Begin by identifying your 'ideal', and most 'profitable' customer personas.

Think in detail about all of the features, descriptions and attributes of your target, 'ideal' customer. Imagine them in your mind's eye walking in through the door. Note their age, gender and what they are wearing. What devices do they use to connect digitally. Imagine their typical day. What time's during the day are they most likely to be connected digitally. Think first thing in the morning, on the commute, during the morning, over lunchtime, in the afternoon, on the commute home, during the evening, last thing before sleep. These are all patterns you can test. Note how socially connected are they in the real world and online. If they only have small social networks then traditional marketing may still work well for them. Add into the sheet which supermarket they buy their groceries from, where the go on holiday, what brand and type of car they drive, and what other brands you would associate with them. This can help to align your tone of voice and imagery with their preferences. What else makes this persona different to the general public. The more detailed their profile the more you can create professional intimacy with them, some way beyond that of your competitors. if you have multiple target customers of different types then repeat this exercise with each one.

What is the first name that comes to mind when you think about your Persona. Give them that name. They are now a real person and you can refer to them as such within your digital content production and marketing. Repeat this process with each Persona you have created.

Thinking deeply about your Persona(s) and what it is that they want. Think beyond the features and benefits of the products and services and aim for what outcomes they are seeking. How will their world be different if they solve their challenges, enjoy your products and services or brand experience. What real world issues or challenges are you solving with them?

It is vital to note precisely what digital tools your Persona(s) use now and potentially into the future. Begin by noting what devices they use, from smartphones and tablets to computers. Think about their social media accounts. Answer honestly based on your analytics, experience or assumptions (which you can test later) rather than what you would like them to use, simply because it's convenient for you. The trick is to go to their places, rather than expect them to come to yours.

Checklist : Define them, find them and listen to them

Because you must not consider your target audience as 'everyone', do you have a forensically clear view of your target customer?

How old is your ideal customer persona? They should be 34 years old, for example, rather than between 25 and 45.

What are the features, descriptions and attributes of your target, 'ideal' customer?

Imagine them walking into the room. What is their gender and what they are wearing?

What devices do they use to connect digitally?

Imagining their typical day. What time's during the day are they most likely to be connected digitally?

How socially connected are they in the real world and online?

Which supermarket do they buy their groceries from?

Where do they go on holiday?

What brand and type of car do they drive?

What other brands you would associate with them? This can help to align your tone of voice and imagery with their preferences.

What else makes this specific persona different to the general public?

Do you have multiple target customers of different types? If yes, then repeat this exercise with each one.

What is the first name that comes to mind when you think about your Persona? Give them that name. They are now a real person.

4.2 OPTIMISE : PERSONAS : BUILD FAITH AND TRUST

Robin Sloan defined stock and flow content to help us to understand the difference between content that becomes legacy (stays in our digital presence) and that which is more transitory and temporary (limited value in the future).

"Flow is the feed. It's the posts and the tweets. It's the stream of daily and sub-daily updates that remind people that you exist."

"Stock is the durable stuff. It's the content you produce that's as interesting in two months (or two years) as it is today. It's what people discover via search. It's what spreads slowly but surely, building fans over time."

There is a trend at present towards disposable content and the networks such as Snapchat are encouraging a high level of transitory content (flow) which is 'in the moment' but of less value, even in a short period of time.

The most savvy marketers are seeing the benefit in balancing both forms of content as they strive for both the regular drip feeding of interesting, current and relevant snippets of content (flow) and the more thought-provoking and sustainable content (stock) which will both stand the test of time and which enhances the quality, durability and credence of their digital footprint in the long term.

Search engines rate both forms of content and especially stock content which benefits from longevity, which we believe is important to the search algorithms.

Tell stories that your persona will remember.

Mark Satterfield said, "Tell stories that people remember". Never a truer word has been spoken, either in face to face sales meetings or online through digital marketing.

The essence of the message is that as human beings we aren't really interested in facts and figures but rather the 'what's in it for me'. So the next time you are blogging, tweeting, calling a prospect or selling in a meeting remember some really important things:

1. People buy people, not products or services - if they like you then you will make the sale, if they don't then no matter how good your offer, they will go elsewhere

2. Customers make their decision before they realise it - sales decisions are made in customers' unconscious minds 5 seconds before their conscious mind kicks in and starts talking facts and figures

3. The best way to tap into the unconscious mind is to engage people with a story - "Before we start, let me tell you what happened to me..." is the ideal way to tap into the unconscious natural curiousity that we all have whether we like it or not

4. You don't have to be a natural storyteller - we are not talking the funniest, scariest or most shocking story telling here, just simply a personal case study or great testimonial story from a client

5 The close is crucial - "So what do you think?" sounds too soft when you read this with your conscious mind but to your unconscious mind at the end of the story the customer will surely want such a great experience and benefits themselves

Telling stories that people remember is a fascinating approach to selling and online marketing that you just might want to give a try. Prospects become customers without even realising it. Has this worked for you?

One of the most recent fashions and something at the heart of the Web 2.0 social media revolution is that of having a company blog . This is now the de facto standard for retaining a two way ongoing relationship with customers and suppliers. A personalised internal view of the organisation through a regularly updated blog can portray the real face of the business and transcend the brand.

Care should be taken to reflect existing brand values at the same time as ensuring that the blog is not perceived as a convenient add-on but rather as an essential communication mechanism delivering value to the reader/contributor.

Importantly, the concept of 'content is king' has been surpassed by 'relevant content is king' where customer-focused and user-specific content drives true value. A simple example is the inclusion of a '?' at the end of a blog or social media comment to invite others to post responses, comments and discussions to what previously might have been just a statement.

This open engagement and stimulation of online conversation through all channels is at the heart of both Web 2.0 and measurable marketing effectiveness.

Once you publish a blog, an email, some news, a website or social media comment, it is immortal and online forever, even if you delete it! There is a huge upside in publishing digital content. From a humble email to interesting blog, from social media chat to a customer case study every time you publish content online you are allowing your messages to pass far and wide, around the globe and back again, touching customers and prospects on the way.

It is said that a key benefit of digital media over printed is that if you make a mistake then rather than have to scrap that pile of 10,000 printed brochures you can simply make your correction on your computer screen and click the 'update' button. Well that is partially true but you should not take this for granted and here are some reasons why.

Look at Twitter. As soon as you have tweeted a message to your followers, even if you then instantly click 'delete' your original post will likely have been picked up by content aggregators, websites taking your content feed and even a search engine or two that happened to be looking in your direction at that moment. The delete button may give the appearance that your content is gone but it is not, it is still out there.

Think about email and e-newsletters. You send out your monthly newsletter containing a quote that your customer then decides they would rather not see in public so you press recall, or attempt to edit the central copy on your content management system. But it is already too late.

Your e-newsletter has been stored locally in folders on recipients' computers or perhaps printed out. Worse still it is already been forwarded on to colleagues and friends, compounding the problem.

Imagine your website, the whole thing, not just a page or two. In years to come your competitors, customers and prospects will be able to see what you did, said and offered back in the day. You think you have moved on with a beautiful sparkly new site taking in your expensive new branding and company logo. But do a search and look beyond page one and you will see all sorts of 'cached' content taking you back years and years. Is what you see what you would like people to remember you by? You really have no choice unless you start planning today what people are going to see tomorrow.

This is the importance of content, the fuel of your digital marketing activities and at the heart of your strategy to build faith and trust in your customer persona's perception of you.

Checklist : Build faith and trust

What does your persona really want from you?

Beyond the features and benefits of the products and services, what outcomes they are seeking from you?

How will their world be different if they solve their challenges, enjoy your products and services or brand experience?

Precisely what digital tools and devices do your target personas use, from smartphones and tablets to computers?

Based on your analytics, experience or assumptions (which you can test later) which social networks do your personas use?

What real world issues or challenges are you solving for them?

What are the three most important things you can do to build your customers' trust?

What are you going to do today to improve the level of faith and trust your target persona has in you?

4.3 : OPTIMISE : PERSONAS : POWER OF INFLUENCERS

Market to Influencers as well as Decision Makers

In every business transaction, whether business to business (B2B) or business to consumer (B2C) there are a host of individuals involved and not just the eventual decision maker or the most obvious person holding the purse strings.

We call it the Decision Making Unit (DMU) and it's crucial to really delve in and understand who is influencing who, when, how and why.

An influencer is anyone who has a relationship (personal or business) with the decision maker and who's opinions, views, and role can alter or affect the thoughts of the decision maker. They can be highly influential and especially from the perspective of their relationship with the decision maker.

For example, in the family unit, the husband may hand over the credit card for payment of an item for the home but the wife is likely to have a significant opinion that will influence the choice or product or retailer.

In the business decision making unit, the budget holder may be influenced by their immediate senior, the board of directors, the finance department and their peers.

The key to understanding the influencers is in the different language they will understand when you communicate your product or service. If you solely focus on the features, benefits and outcomes associated with your decision maker and ignore the influencers then you are offering just one flavour of your proposition. If you understand that different influencers have a different agenda then you can begin to offer truly customer-focused messages and communications to each persona. A simple example is in the business development process. If you talk to your customer they have some clear needs you will solve. The influencer in finance wants to know the return on investment (ROI) and cost. The influencer in human resources will want to know any potential impact on the people in the business, processes and potentially staff recruitment. The influencer in production will want to know if there will be any required changes to systems or technologies and in sales they will want to know if there are any potentials for business development.

Focusing on multiple perspectives and adapting your marketing approach to satisfy the needs of the influencers will ensure that when the decision maker searches for support in their decision from others around the business then they are met with positive and agreeable answers. In business to consumer (B2C) focus not only on the obvious person with the cash, but also those who are likely to be impacted on their decision, the partner, the children, the parents, the friends.

Everyone has a part to play as you build your brand in your target markets.

Let your competitors go after the decision maker and fight it out, whilst you subtly and cleverly add value to everyone else involved. Influence the influencers and watch the rewards come in your direction.

Checklist : Power of influencers

In a perfect world, who would you like to work with as a positive influence on your target customer personas?

What would you like your influencers to do for you, what should they say and where should they say it?

How will your influencers be perceived by your target customer persona?

How will you know when you are seeing a positive outcome from the efforts of your influencers?

Where and how will you take the next steps to engage with your target influencers?

5.1 OPTIMISE : CUSTOMER JOURNEY : BUILD AWARENESS

All digital marketing should have a clear and defined purpose; to encourage and convince our personas to carry out an action, behave differently or engage with us.

At each step of their engagement with us we should be leading them carefully and comfortably to the next step. Ultimately we want them to reach the point of conversion.

When this objective is achieved, and they have converted our persona has moved from being a prospect (a potential or lead) to being a customer.

The buying behaviour process, and it is a process, is defined as the 'decision process and acts of individuals involved in buying and using products or services' (Dibb et al 2001)

There are five key phases in the process:

Need Recognition

Information Search

Evaluation of Alternatives

Purchase Decision

Post-Purchase Evaluation of Decision

These five stages have been fundamental to traditional marketing planning and continue to be important considerations in offline purchases.

When the customer moves online the five stages take on a new lease of life and control in the process passes significantly to the customer as the breadth of options and ease of access to information grows exponentially on the internet.

Need Recognition - the first step in the process where the prospective customer recognises they have a need to solve a challenge or a problem or to enhance an element of their world. This is either driven by the prospective customer themselves or by the marketer who proactively advertises (paid content) or publishes relevant and timely content online (owned content).

Information Search - the internet opens up a global smorgasbord of information from commercial sources and public sources as well as private individuals' sources (those who have already been through a similar purchase process).

Evaluation of Alternatives - a key part of the evaluation of alternatives (and one that is not so readily available in the offline buying process) is that of seeking advocates", reviewers and influencers' opinions of the alternatives available. This is often terms 'earned content'.

Purchase Decision - the purchase decision, or conversion point as the individual transitions from being a prospect, into a customer, can be complex and can be influenced by the attitudes of others and situational factors, timing and anticipated outcomes from the purchase.

Post-Purchase Evaluation of Decision - in offline purchases it can often be the case of being individually, either satisfied or dis-satisfied with the purchase. Online, things can be more complex, as the customer posts reviews, comments and feelings about their purchase and then receives instant feedback that may or may not support their decision. This in turn has an impact on how they feel about their decision and whether or not they would advocate the product or service and whether or not they would repeat their decision or take another, in the future.

The customers' reaction will have a direct impact on the organisation's confidence, strategy and future tactical activities. To implement effective marketing, the company needs to continually listen to understand influences on what, where and how their customers buy. Understanding the influences helps drive continuous improvement and to predict the effectiveness of future marketing activities.

It is crucial to understand the context within which the customer receives and interprets marketing messages. The context will include factors such as: culture, social influence, personal preferences, and psychological factors like motivation, perception, learning, beliefs and attitudes.

As we have eluded to before, each different customer persona being targeted will have very different contexts in which they are interpreting the marketing they encounter.

Enduring involvement is an ongoing interest in a product or product area. This is particularly common in hobbies and past times. For example a keen fisherman my spend a lot of time reading about the best fishing equipment even if he cannot afford to buy it.

Situation involvement demonstrates a temporary interest because of immediate circumstances, for example 'it is raining and I need an umbrella' or 'I am about to go on a beach holiday and I need to know what to take'.

Low Involvement occurs in routine purchases which do not generate very much customer interest. An example would be buying bleach to clean the kitchen floor.

Where Does Your Customers' Journey Begin?

I was waiting in a long queue to be served by an organisation who shall remain nameless.

It was a busy lunchtime queue as customers of all shapes and sizes made good use of their break from work to use the service. The retail counter was well staffed with happy, smiley people. Each representative, clearly tasked with improving their customer engagement, took time out during the sales process to chat about the weather, comment on the customer's clothes and pass the time of day.

At the point of purchase this may well have increased the level of engagement and customer satisfaction but in an ever lengthening queue of those not yet in position at the counter it became increasingly frustrating.

So what was happening here for the customer journey?

Management had clearly given the staff a task of increasing the personal engagement in every transaction. Each approach to the counter was greeted with a smile and what on the surface appeared to be great service. However, what the management and staff had collectively failed to realise, is that by doubling the time spent in the queue, each customer's satisfaction had dropped to a level below normal, and the added value they were seeing at the counter only brought them back, if at all, to the original level.

With a slower throughput of customers and probably some people seeing the length of the queue and then going elsewhere, the cost of time and resource is likely to have increased beyond the positive benefit of increased customer engagement.

So the moral of the story is that whilst there may have been great intentions to increase customer satisfaction, the reality is that without considering the full extent of the customer journey (which begins way before your customer is in front of you) you may ultimately be disappointed with the outcome.

Where do your customers' journeys begin?

Supporting the broader concept of the customer journey, we have a chance to define the process of the digital sales conversion funnel.

This is a step by step process that demonstrates the digital tools required to take an initial encounter with a prospect through to the eventual sale to them of a product or service.

The prospect becomes a customer when they purchase or behave in such a way that the marketer has defined as providing their organisation with value. This might be a financial value coming from a product sale, or it could be a change in behaviour, in the case of, for example, a government department encouraging a community to support a cause or act in a specific way.

The term 'sales conversion' is widely known and used. Our sales funnel, filled at the top with incoming website visitors for example then sees a drop-off in numbers at each click as they navigate through the website to an eventual goal. Improving each step of the customer journey process allows small enhancements to create large incremental performance changes and significant improvements to the end output at the base of the funnel (the conversion).

Conversion funnels also provide the opportunity to test, or A/B

Testing. This is very simple and yet powerful and allows us to continually improve our customer journey. For example, if we have two versions of a web page, with perhaps two different offers – maybe one of the campaigns is centred on low price but the other on quality. We call the first 'A' and the second 'B'. These two pages are created and the server is told to alternate the viewing: so A goes to the first visitor, B to the second, A to the third and so on. Then a conversion funnel is created for both options and through Google Analytics (our website monitoring tool) we can see the difference.

This is simple but effective experimentation. Other more detailed testing can include MVA which means Multi-Variate Analysis, and goes beyond testing two versions (bi-variate analysis) and tests many aspects.

Checklist : Build awareness

Which tools will you use at the start of your target customer personas' journey to steadily increase their faith and trust in you?

List every point at which your prospective could have first encountered you? Include real world (offline) communication points?

Word of Mouth and Google Search are invariably included at this initial stage, plus advertising, events, calls or email campaigns?

From each of these initial touch points, what is the next point, and then the next. Note step by step where you want them to go?

Can you differentiate between reactive tools and self-serve tools? The former is where the prospective customer just happens upon you and your messages. Seeing an advertisement is a good example. The latter is where they actively seek out a company like yours. Google search is a good example because they have already identified a need to be solved. A prospective customer arriving at your door in a reactive mindset will need more hand holding through the initial steps of their journey than one arriving in a self-serve mindset because they have already identified the hope stage in their hope-faith-trust stages.

Do all steps eventually route towards the Conversion point in your customers' journey?

Towards the end of the awareness phase and just before conversion, does your prospective customer see testimonials and case studies?

What will be the best tools and channels to help you communicate these?

What tools and activities can you eliminate and scale-up today to improve awareness in the eyes of your target customer persona?

5.2 OPTIMISE : CUSTOMER JOURNEY : CONVERT WITH CONFIDENCE

Up-Selling, Cross-Selling and Back-Selling

To cross-sell to a customer you simply see what they have purchased and then sell them appropriate other products and services that are related to the original purchase. To up-sell to a customer you look at their purchase and then over time increase the customer's financial value to your business by encouraging them to purchase new versions, ongoing upgrades or additional elements of the original product or service.

There is an often missed third sell which can be both ignored or mis-understood and this is the more subtle 'back-sell'.

Consider, as an example, a law firm who takes on a new client in order to deliver legal conveyancing services for them as they move home. Ordinarily the firm would then think about cross-selling in the future by offering services like wills and probate. These being future services the client may need. In many ways we are all focused on the future and what we can market and sell to customers in front of us.

But pause for a moment and consider the client and where they have come from. Are there services you have to offer, that would have been relevant before they found you? Have they missed a product or service that you could go back and sell to in-fill essential things they should have? In the law firm example it could be related to family legal matters, prenuptial agreements or perhaps employment or commercial services if they have a business.

The way that this is possible is that as well as creating a 'customer journey' for the client, you need to consider their personal lifecycle before they became your customer. By plotting their life stages and then overlaying the products and services you offer at each stage, you align what you do with what they need at specific moments in time. Then you are able to look backward on the timeline to moments before they engaged with you to check with them they have everything they need.

This intimacy with customers is key to truly understanding their needs and acting appropriately at specific times. If you are able to back-sell you will at the same time be creating otherwise missed revenue and thereby generate increased customer lifetime value.

By setting clear objectives right the way through the conversion funnel journey the digital marketer is able to continuously test and improve outcomes in a controlled manner and thereby improve return on investment to the organisation.

So our aim is clear. Step by step hand holding through every step of engagement. In many ways we can call this approach to customer-centric marketing, customer optimisation.

Customer optimisation is actually as important as search engine optimisation (SEO) in terms of the actual experience the customer enjoys after the SEO has worked and brought them to the website for example. These concepts are at the heart of customer relationship management (CRM).

Different things will apply to their experience depending on where they are in their customer journey:

Awareness Stage

The Awareness stage is from the very first point at which the persona ever sees or hears about the business through steps to the point they convert from a prospect, lead or 'just interested' to being a customer. Many marketers think that 'creating brand awareness' is the sole function of digital marketing, but in fact it is just the beginning of the customers' journey.

Through the awareness phase it is vital that the marketer uses suitable digital marketing, and offline, tools relevant to the persona and fuels them with content that engages both emotionally and practically, stimulating them to move to the next step in the journey. Through this process the aim is to turn the persona's hope into faith they have arrived in the right place and then to trusting such that they are willing to go over the line and convert.

Conversion Stage

The conversion is the point (defined by the marketer in advance) where the customer fully commits to the brand, company, product or service. They may purchase, engage or behave in such a way that the marketer sees as providing value to their plan. Everything in the awareness stage should eventually point to the conversion point.

Following the pattern of moving the prospective customer from their hope to faith and then trust will ensure they have reasons to buy rather than being sold to. This is crucial for their confidence in passing over the line to becoming a customer.

Checklist : Convert with confidence

At the end of the Awareness Phase are you successfully and consistently converting your prospects' awareness into a customer?

What proportion of those interested or aware, eventually convert into customers?

What can you do today to improve the conversion rate?

What tools, digital and offline/traditional, will assist your customer conversions from both your and their perspectives?

What customer data will you collect and where will it be held?

How you can interrogate your customer data to analyse what you might do more of and what you might wish to filter out in the future?

What steps the customer should experience immediately after their conversion?

What do they receive from you, what should they do and where should they go?

Are you collecting information specific to the conversion or purchase and in line with your planned future marketing contact intentions?

What will you improve today to your conversion phase of the customer journey?

5.3 OPTIMISE : CUSTOMER JOURNEY : RETAIN TO SUSTAIN YOUR BUSINESS

After the point of conversion the digital marketer's fun really begins. The majority of value the marketer will enjoy from digital communication comes in the retention stage; keeping the existing customer engaged, satisfied and happy.

In this stage we need to ensure that existing customers are not just old customers, but actively up-buying and cross-buying and behaving as loyal and highly valuable channels to market. The content strategy should demonstrate that the organisation is current, relevant and informed, adding value on a timely and ongoing basis to the customer.

Optimisation must ensure it addresses all three stages for the benefit of the search engine and also the customer experience.

Ultimate Customer Journey

One of the most important elements in customer experience is what we define as the Customer Journey. This is the end to end experience from the first moment of engagement to the point of lifelong advocacy where the customer is so engaged and loyal they perceive no need to go anywhere else for product or service.

Defining your customers' journeys is vital to ensure best fit of your service provision with their needs and desires.

If you are seeking a real world example that encapsulates not only the initial promise but through the real world experience, then fly into Copenhagen airport and navigate with ease, to and from the centre of the city.

Before travelling you can navigate to your chosen App Store and search for the Copenhagen Metro Mobilbilletter app. This is your passport from airport, to, around and back from the city.

Step by step from Arrivals lounge to the clean and airy Metro platform you are guided by the clearest signs and through tempting food halls and cafes en route.

Arriving at the platform it is likely you will have already opened *the app which automatically locates your device by GPS and begins the zone pricing options as your departure station. Select a destination by name if you know it, or by clicking on a map roughly in the direction you want. If you know the name of your hotel or destination the app not only automatically buys the correct ticket and advises the best route but also gives you a short guide for your onward journey of the time and distance you will need to walk at the other end.*

All very helpful and stress-free until you add in the timing of the arrival of the next driverless train, which arrives at your platform to the second. There is no waiting for late arrival or delayed journeys, you know exactly at what time you will arrive. This customer journey keeps getting better.

It does more than it claims when you consider how clean, airy and full of space the train carriages are. No graffiti, stains or litter, this is clarity of purpose and precision of delivery.

So how can you take this example of a real world customer journey into helping you improve the service you provide to your customers?

Plot the Basics - begin by drawing the end to end customer journey, but first consider just the basics. Think of all the very simple things that provide the minimal, base level of service that your customers require.

Add Value - add in at various steps some real added-value elements that provide more of a 'Wow!' Factor and make your customers sit up, notice and feel impressed.

Wrap Around Service - throughout the journey include a wrapper of service excellence. Brief all staff throughout the organisation that they all have a part to play in delighting the customer and empower them to do so. If you have a driver-less train, make sure your computer is well programmed! Your people are one of your unique sales propositions (USPs) if you use them wisely.

You will know when you have your Customer Journey just right, not because you feel it is, but because your customers tell you it is. If nobody is advocating how great you are then there is more to be done. If you cannot see the customer experience you provide as an end to end, integrated Customer Journey, then there is more to be done. If you cannot measure, to a granular level of detail, everything you do in your customer communications, then there is more to be done.

Customer Journeys that are shared and written about are the ones that are working.

Checklist : Retain to sustain your business

When plotting the retention phase, what tools will aid the drip feeding of engaging content to your customers?

How will you ensure you remain front of mind, ready for the next purchase, sales renewal or perhaps customer service request?

When and how frequently is the optimum amount to engage with your existing customers?

How will you stimulate and encourage loyalty leading to advocacy and further sales and commitment from your customers?

What is your current customer lifetime value and what steps can you take today to improve it?

6.1 OPTIMISE : CONTENT STRATEGY : RULE OF THIRDS

Striking balance in digital content is an absolute necessity to avoid hearing the adage "Oh they always talk about themselves."

Without wishing to insult an entire industry, in fact it was where I started my career, but the recruitment sector is possibly the worst example of missing the point when it comes to balance and maintaining audience interest. We have all seen some recruitment agency Twitter accounts. Job advertisements after job advertisements and nothing more. If I am not seeking a new job, why would I be interested in following?

However if the agency talked about their team members, the charity work they do, shared careers advice and perhaps salary surveys or events in my local city, then they are adding significantly more value and reasons to stay engaged and I am more likely to continue to follow them. When the time comes that I'm seeking a new role they could be the first recruiters I turn to because they have been consistently on my personal radar.

This is where we can begin to think about the Digital Content Rule of Thirds.

I have seen my Rule work without failing in every sector and industry I can think of. I have shared my Rule with literally thousands of people through workshops and events. The likes of Hootsuite and Hubspot have blogged about it to share it far and wide. In all this time and with the largest of research samples I can confidently say that not a single person has come back to me to say it hasn't worked for them. It just seems to work and I'm confident that if you practice it then it will work for you and your business too.

Three really does seem to be a magic number. There is a Rule of Thirds in photography and art. Three is a magic number in nature and throughout history we have seen three of many important and sacred things.

Digital content is no different and the Rule of Thirds can be applied to all sorts of published works from email newsletters to blogs and from social media to news pages on websites.

The first thing to clarify is that we aren't talking about squeezing each third into everything we publish. It's about striking a balance over multiple posts or articles. If you were to look back at your last 30 tweets for example, then 10 would be one of the Thirds, 10 another Third and 10 the final Third. So clearly not the same as trying to put all three Thirds into a single tweet which in itself has a limited number of characters to play with.

So let's find out about each of the Thirds in the Digital Content Rule of Thirds.

One Third of everything you publish is Personal, one Third is Point, one Third is Promote; the three Ps of digital content, if you like.

Personal

This Third is all about sharing content that helps your audience to get to know you. It might be getting to know you personally, your team or perhaps an appropriate 'face of the organisation'. Too many companies try to use their CEO or Managing Director, but is that person really the one who your target Personas want to engage with? If the answer is yes then that's great. But if not then find someone who would resonate more freely and readily in the Persona's view.

I spoke to a distribution company who decided to use their Junior Warehouse Assistant as the face of the business because it gave a more authentic, grass roots, view of the business and this was consistent with the style of brand and tone of voice they were establishing with their customers. The real behind the scenes messages conveyed so much more about the business and its operations than a tight, sterile, corporate message.

Getting to know the people in the business is so key to help establish competitive advantage. Especially in commoditised industries where there is little differentiation, the characters and uniqueness of the individuals behind the brand, products and services are a core competency, memorable, difficult to replicate and vital to establishing the long term, sustainable and loyal relationships that we all seek.

Point

The Point Third is about signposting to other people's content rather than your own. This pointing is crucial to striking the balance in digital content and especially social media.

Third party content can be a rich source of ideas, opportunities and inspiration, not only for yourself but for the Personas with whom you wish to engage.

A great idea is to set up Twitter lists into which you add accounts who post great tweets. You don't have to follow these accounts to add them to your lists and you can choose to make your lists public or private. When you have this stream of great content that you've selected because it is relevant and interesting for your target Personas, you can select occasional links and retweet or publish short articles containing them.

If you intimately know your Personas you'll know the kinds of subjects they'll find most interesting. Remember this content is not about you and your products and it might be very different to your sector altogether. Think of your key Personas' interests, lifestyle and aspirations.

As an example, when I first created my marketing consultancy we knew that Nicky, one of our top Personas, loved our remote working lifestyle. So when we took an extra long lunch to enjoy the local mountain bike trails we would share ways that Nicky could blend her work and interests much in the same way that we do. The result was that Nicky has remained tuned into our world and whenever she needs marketing support, we were at the front of her mind.

The Point Third is vital because it's unpredictable. I like to think of it as 'free stuff'. Free because it won't take you long to locate and share it. Stuff because it can get quite random and unpredictable. This unpredictability is key because it ensures your audience aren't quite sure what is coming next. This means they are always alert to your content when you publish it and this tees up the final Third perfectly.

Pointing is content curation.

Promote

Because by now your audience is alert to your every post because you have been sharing a lot to help to get to know you, and valuable, quite random, but highly relevant content, then they are ready for your final Third, the overt Promote.

If anyone tells you that you should not use social media for promotion then they clearly haven't been striking an appropriate balance ofÂ getting to know them coupled with valuable third party content curation. If they have then their audience is ready and willing to accept promotion.

Everyone you are connected with knows you have messages, products and services that you would like them to be aware of and by the time you arrive at your final Third it's time to be overt with your promotion because you have earned it.

Knowing your Personas as you do, you will have found appropriate marketing channels, messages and communication styles to establish mutually beneficial engagement. You can now use these relationships to promote what you want. Your Personas are ready.

Remember with the Rule of Thirds you don't have to squeeze each of the Thirds into a single article or tweet, it's simply about balancing them across your wider communications, check back over the last dozen articles or tweets and you should see one third Personal, one third Point, one third Promote.

Do You Stand Out?

"We can't see the wood for the trees" is a traditional saying that typifies how many organisations in many industries experience everyday life.

It's a self fulfilling prophecy as you continually try to outperform the opposition with just little tweaks and tuning to your products and services that look, feel and sound much like they do.

It has always been this way and you could argue this is how market sectors and industries have evolved and become defined.

First we have a market leader and the inevitable market challenger. You know the types. Big players; number one and number two in the sector. Most people have heard of them and they tend to lead the way when it comes to share of voice, budgets and turnover.

Then we have the market followers. More often than not described as the meek and the mild who are in a continuous state of playing catch-up. Trying to spot them in the midst of the noise is a challenge but that's fine because they only really get attention when a customer wants to compare prices or terms. The decision has already been made.

But then there are the canny, sometimes fleet-of-foot specialists, the market niche players. Typically smaller in scale but adaptable, innovative and flexible. You might find you can get something a little special from them if you can take the time to find them. This can come at a price because by definition they are probably offering customers something they can't get elsewhere.

The difference you see is that the ones most in control are the market niche players because if they have something special to offer, something small, discrete and profitable, then they can control their own destiny rather than having to continuously play the game of beating the competition. Their challenge is to stand out and be accessible, to cut through the noise.

So whichever market positioning you have decided to take… is it right for your organisation and strategy? And vitally, do you stand out?

Checklist : Rule of Thirds Content Strategy

What content can you share from a Personal perspective to help your target customer get to know you?

Where and what content from third parties can you use to Point to that will resonate and add value for your customers' experience?

What relevant Promote content can you schedule, to enable the overt sales messages to support your business

development?

Who else will help you to fuel your customers' journey in each of the Thirds?

Do you have an equal balance of Personal, Point, Promote content and how will you sustain new ideas for content?

Where will you store new ideas for content that you can use in the future?

6.2 OPTIMISE : CONTENT STRATEGY : BECOME CURRENT, RELEVANT AND INFORMED

How to Create an Elevator Pitch

You have no time to go into detail, and in those brief moments you need to encapsulate everything that is good about you and your business. You need to share the ethos, the aims, the values and style and perhaps a little about the products and services you offer. You could also share something very different, perhaps a statement about the outcomes your customers benefit from by working with you.

A key to the most effective elevator pitches is to consider your augmented product. The question is "What's Your Augmented Product" ? An augmented product is a service wrapper. It's not your product or your core service and what it does. It is much more about the less tangible wrapper around all of this. In other words it's those little details which give you a competitive edge. Things you do beyond what it is you do, that provide that 'wow' or that little bit extra, that nobody else does.

The augmented product might be a minuscule detail but it's the one that you regularly hear back from your customers that they like and value the most. The little difference. Your elevator pitch can be like everyone else but with a little thought and care you can increase the intrigue and engagement level by talking more than features and benefits and outcomes of what you do and think more about how you are different and why.

My elevator pitch could be that I am a marketing consultant who works with customers to improve their marketing. But that puts me right in the middle of a group of some 1,000,000 other marketing consultants across the planet. I would rather focus on something like the fact I help people to communicate more effectively by helping them to turn their chaos into clarity.

When I say this I see people smile, because I think they know that I understand some of their professional pain. That is my augmented product, the service wrapper around the varied and numerous marketing tools at my disposal.

Elevator Pitch on Steroids

Imagine you are going to an event, conference or seminar and thinking you'll be able to sit near the back to quietly absorb information and ideas. On arrival you are ushered into a quiet corner to be invited to take centre stage because the scheduled presenter is unable to make it.

How would this make you feel? If the answer includes one or more of the following then you have work to do:
1. It would strike the fear of god into me
2. Where would I start
3. I need a powerpoint presentation to hide behind
4. Speaking to a packed audience isn't my thing
5. People wouldn't be interested in what I have to say

The current trend to becoming a Social Business takes on many forms. It's not just about being active online, contributing to Linkedin Discussion Groups or constantly tweeting. It's about having a clear understanding not only of how to succinctly get across the messages that are most important about your products and services but also the idea of giving a little something away for free with the aim of inspiring interest, gaining trust and enhancing credibility.

It was a little exercise I tried yesterday evening when presented with exactly this situation. Thrust into the limelight on stage (a place I have to admit I do enjoy after many years leading training sessions and workshops) as one of two people who drew (as I see it) the long straw.

So what did I talk about? The subject matter that I was intending to listen to had the scheduled presenter been able to make it.

But for me it was about positioning a single idea, in my case our magic Rule of Thirds, in the minds of the audience. Rather than spout on about how Viper Marketing had done this, and achieved that, far better to spin your elevator pitch in a language the audience understands and to give a little something away for free that they can try when they get home.

It's not about being clever or intelligent, a great networker or public speaker. It's about having some core subjects in your toolkit that you can wheel out and share with no notice. You really do get what you give and for me it has been proven since the event by the number of high quality invitations to connect via Linkedin with people in the audience.

It's always 'work in progress'. Anyone who thinks they have a Social Business that's complete, is missing the point. It's an evolutionary situation that you never crack but with a little planning, foresight and luck you can hopefully come somewhere close.

So I challenge you…. take 15 minutes and see if you can talk about what you do, in a language I'd understand, so that I understand what you do, without you talking about your products and services.

Checklist : Become current, relevant and informed

How does your target customer persona currently perceive your digital content, frequency of publishing and relevance to them?

If competitors are focusing elsewhere, can you get tactical and strike by filling any potentially profitable gaps in the market?

If commentators, bloggers, influencers or the media are talking about specific subjects that resonate with your target persona, can you include your opinion and add value to the conversation?

What 'thought leadership' subjects can you use, share and blog, to become synonymous with?

What changes will you make today to become perceived as current, relevant and informed?

6.3 OPTIMISE : CONTENT STRATEGY : CREATION, CURATION, DOCUMENTATION

"It only has impact when it's human" Robert Fox, Evening Standard.

A simple sentence but so poignant in today's content rich, social business, digitally driven, economically testing world.

Imagine social networking without a human element to what you talk about? There are examples of social media profile pictures of company logos or worse still no image at all. How little do you want to engage with them?

You visit a website that shows just dry, dull product information and technical product photography. How much more engaging would it be to see someone just like you using and benefiting from the product or service?

News stories in the media that talk about numbers, statistics, facts and detail but without how it made those affected feel, think and react, sound like white noise. You will never remember them.

No matter how you cut it, what technology you are using, however good your case studies and testimonials, how competitive your pricing and marketing, at the end of the day it really does only have impact when it's human.

When you begin to create your content strategy it's vital that you think of it as strategy, a longer term view aiming to a clear destination point, rather than an immediate quick fix. This is real future-proofing because it stimulates consistency and focus rather than the equivalent of pandering to trending topics.

As part of this future-proofing, a key decision in the process is whether to create, curate and/or document your content.

Content creation is the process of writing, producing and publishing your own content.

Content curation is the collaborative process of using third party content in full or in part to supplement your own.

Content documentation is creation, but at a micro level, documenting processes and internal activities in your organisation and providing the intriguing 'fly on the wall' ongoing documentary, that satisfies the inherent curiosity in the human psyche.

It's most likely that your content strategy will include all three elements, because it needs to satisfy the balance of the Rule of Thirds (see the later section) which emphasises that your target audience will benefit from and be seeking to get to know you, be shown interesting third party content and then accept you will want to promote some things to them.

Remember, whichever mix of content styles you choose, it's all about story-telling. Your target customer persona will enjoy and engage with stories far longer and more detailed than you would anticipate. People are curious and intrigued. Feed their appetite.

Checklist : Creation, curation, documentation and story-telling

What is your Unique Selling Proposition (USP) that is the bedrock of your digital content?

Have you created a strong, engaging and clear statement of the unique value that your messages, products and services add to your customers' worlds?

Is your USP (ideally you may have more than one) also your core competence? You have many capabilities, as do your competitors, but what one capability is your core competence, that nobody else does and that adds most value to your customers.

What opportunities are available to enhance your digital activities? This could include upcoming new product or service launches, events and exciting news.

What third party content sources will form a key part of your ongoing content strategy by way of curation?

In documenting and story-telling, who else will help you create, edit and publish engaging content and in what form?

7.1 DELIVER : WEBSITE : DIGITAL HUB

The customer journey can be seen as a digital hub.

Imagine a bicycle wheel. It has a hub at the centre and spokes linking it to the outer rim and tyres, where contact is made with the surroundings. Effective social networking and digital marketing is very similar and, if implemented, helps to filter out irrelevant marketing tools and prioritise the most important, providing a clarity of experience and, importantly, a central point at which to encourage conversations, engagement and transactions.

Depending on your strategy you may put social media, or even perhaps a traditional offline
tool like the telephone, at the hub. More often though it's likely your website will be the hub of your digital marketing communications strategy and as such, everything should encourage people back, again and again by accurate and timely signposting of articles and content held there.

Marketing Communications is Signposting the Customer Journey

Present a website, run a campaign, send a brochure, meet face to face, engage at an event, chat on social media, speak at a conference; Whatever your marketing communications, there is one thing that's certain. Allow your customers to choose how, when and where they engage with you and there's no knowing where they'll end up. I would bet my house that they will end up somewhere inconvenient to you and to them.

Marketing communications is all about choreography. Helping a customer to travel step by step through a carefully integrated set of experiences is key to them ending up in the right place that adds value to them and to you.

Without clear signposting at every step of engagement they may make uninformed choices at best and at worst leave the journey all together for fear of ending up down some dead end alley.

Try this on your website if you don't believe me. Create some clear buttons and links that click through to a specific page and from that page take away any option to travel deeper or further into their navigation. The removal of a clear next step signpost will result in them halting with a bemused look on their face and then pressing the back button or re-searching for what they were initially seeking.

It is all so simple. Whenever you want a customer to move to the next step, create a clear sign that takes them there. You wouldn't expect to navigate around a new city in your car or on foot without some indication of your journey map and marketing navigation is the same.

In marketing terms we call this the customer journey and at each step the sign, or call to action, must clearly lead the way and eventually to an appropriate destination.

Take your own customers' journey yourself and see how it looks from their perspective? Do you need to start putting up some new or better signs?

You need to decide what is at the hub of your digital communications, online marketing and social networking. Where are you trying to direct customers, suppliers and partners? Is it to your website? Is it to specific social networks? Is it to your regular blog? With one element carefully positioned as the core of your communications everything else falls into place and knows its role.... to feed people into the hub.

Strategically it is vital you decide this carefully depending on what your overall objectives are. If it is to have more conversations with potential customers then perhaps your hub is one of your social networks, such as Facebook or LinkedIn, where you can engage with your targets on their terms and in their comfort zone. If your goal is to educate partners about your products and services you might need to drive them to particular pages on your website, in which case all of your digital marketing activity needs to point inwards to these.

Whilst the 'old days' of brochure-style website stereotypes are long since passed for most organisations, care must be taken to avoid the 'corporate brochure' – placing text and images from the brochure online as well as overt selling when the user is seeking an interactive 'relationship' experience. Out of date information or 'page in development' must be avoided at all costs. Visitors are unlikely to return to unfinished or 'in development' web sites.

One of the key ways of enhancing a website is to let it grow and evolve by treating it as a member of staff:

- Give it a job description – a reason for being part of the team
- Invite it to team meetings – talk to it and listen to it
- Give it some tasks and objectives – then you will know if it is performing
- Do an annual review – if it were a person you would, so why not take time out with it
and see if it is really doing what it should
- Keep it in the office conversation – listen to everything it tells you and respond accordingly

Under Development : Please Come Back Soon

There was a large scaffolding hoarding recently covering a building renovation in Westminster and it made me wonder about the old habit digitally of placing holding statements and 'coming soon' banners in place of what should really be there.

In the early days of the internet we had more time, we were more patient and the concept of a digital customer journey was in its infancy. There wasn't a problem with a company having what was called a 'brochure website', a digital translation of their printed product brochure on a computer screen.

Those days are gone and today it's about always-on, seamless customer journeys linking the needs of the customer with the provision of excellent service, whenever it is required. So where does the 'we are not currently available but please come back later' fit? Well in my view it doesn't.

The Back button on your browser instantly provides a link to a competitor website which will likely be open and available for business. No matter how well you dress up the renovation or the empty shell you are building, it's about limiting these empty customer experiences to the minimal time possible, or perhaps and more appropriately, providing a suitable alternative in the meantime.

Whilst the well dressed scaffolding hoarding provided a visually acceptable alternative to the works happening behind it, there is no hiding from the truth it wasn't as good as the finished product.

So the next time you cut a link in your otherwise integrated customer experience, see if you can find a suitable alternative to keep everything live and available. Your customers will thank you.

Too many businesses see their website as 'just another marketing tool' and a chore. Think of recruiting it into your team of people and it will take on a whole new lease of life. Traditional improvement techniques like web analytics, search engine optimisation and social networking are important, but to truly bring your website to life, treat it as you would expect to be treated yourself.

With website development, in most cases and as we know, the importance of 'mobile first', less is definitely more. Take for example www.google.com, and care should be taken to balance style with content. It is also imperative that navigation within the web site is intuitive and effective with minimal numbers of 'mouse clicks' to move between zones. Once the web presence has been established, the next consideration is to drive people towards it. This is often described as UX or User Experience and is an inherent part of the construction of your customers' journeys.

When plotting the UX a useful phenomenon to keep in front of mind is Bounce Rate. Bounce occurs when a visitor clicks onto a website, scans the landing page, decides that the product service/information is not relevant and immediately clicks away. Bounce is a problem that is always going to occur but if the visitor has come to the web page via paid advertising for (Pay Per Click (PPC) advertising) then a bounce is a completely wasted cost. Therefore it is vital to measure, and understand Bounce Rate as part of any marketing activity to demonstrate return on investment (ROI).

The company website is the most mature field of on-line marketing and historically one of the most important digital marketing tools. For the vast majority of online marketing the website is the chosen destination for customers and is the single most valuable piece of digital real estate you will ever own. This is the one thing over which you have complete control and can measure all of the activity on it.

SEO Tips : The Wall of Expectation

Search engine results be they on Google, Bing, Yahoo or others is all about domination of key search phrases that your target customers are using to find products, services and businesses like yours.

To achieve multiple positions in search engine results we have to think about our content from a multitude of perspectives.

As everyone knows, people now search using words, images and video so we are already clear that by having different media our chances of search engine success will be enhanced.

But it's also about creating page after page of great links in the search engine results and everything pointing back to us.

Proactively we have our customer journeys, through which we choreograph our customers' experience step by step, and this means that specific website pages and social networks are used consciously to create this route map. But by limiting ourselves to using just the digital marketing tools in the customers journeys we may be allowing our competitors to sneak in to one or more of the search results positions on a page which if we plan it, we can be dominating.

So it pays to be using and publishing to, even if just occasionally, a broad range of the popular social networks, so that we can dominate key search phrases by including them there, in our content as well. This is a more reactive use of digital content which some could argue is an attempt to competitively dupe the search engines into thinking that our publishing is stronger and more widely distributed than it is.

To eliminate this argument it's all about content quality. By publishing relevant, current and inspirational content we create a Wall of Expectation which will entice our visitors to click on our links to find out more and to potentially enter into the customer journey we have choreographed for them. Such content may include a mix of engaging testimonials, quotes, statistics and things that they won't find elsewhere.

This does create an expectation of a great end result in the mind of the visitor but that's exactly what will challenge us to become every stronger in how we plan and deliver our marketing communications.

As technologies have developed websites have evolved from

the early basic 'brochure' style, static websites through transactional retail sites and are now much more interactive with each customer being able to witness a different, customised site; in essence, the ultimate customer journey.

Websites can operate in many different ways, as end points, launchpads, micro-sites and transactional sites.

End points are websites which users reach via searches and then complete their transaction at that site. E-commerce websites are classic end point sites as their core aim is to capture the user and get them to buy.

However some information sites may aim to ensure users stay within that site (news.bbc.co.uk could be seen to be an end-point). Visits to an end point site are one way to measure the success of a marketing activity though conversion to a sale is also crucial and so the Conversion Ratio of inbound hits to sales is also a vital measure.

Conversion Ratio can be as high as 20% or as low as 1% depending on the market sector and, crucially, the effectiveness of the marketing activity.

Typically an end point website will have a small number of pages/links that will be considered to be the goal. These might be checkout pages or contact/information request forms. Identifying how many customers reach these goal pages and the path they take through the site is crucial.

Launchpads are sites which aim to capture the user early but then direct them onwards to other sites. Search Engines are classic launchpads and earn money from the user leaving the site and going onwards to other content. However some commercial websites could be seen as launchpads. Motor manufacturer sites can be seen as launchpads as their aim it to persuade users to go to a dealership and/or request more information. Launchpads will have many goal pages and locations. Dwell time and customer path is probably of less relevance to these sites however accurate tracking of exits from the site is essential.

Marketing Consequences

Companies large and small the world over typically approach marketing, sales and business development from the perspective of selling the features and benefits of their products and services.

This is all so easy to emulate by competitors who joust and position themselves as having more features or greater benefits. The problems for the target customer is that this is such a lot of noise and confusion. The smallest of incremental differences are shouted from the rooftops but the actual value is often perceived as so small.

The biggest problem is that companies compete on an almost equal footing. The same products, the same features and benefits and in many situations even very similar levels of service, customer attention and support.

In steps the most savvy of marketer or sales person as they begin to add real value and clarity by marketing consequence. The consequence to the customer of not engaging, the consequence to the customer of not buying and the reality of what they'll miss out on if they don't.

The marketing of consequence, by knowing the true value of what you are really selling (not your products or services), helps you to draw out and communicate those essential Unique Sales Propositions (USPs). Do you know what yours are? They could be your people, they could be your innovation, your speed to market, your unique processes...

The consequence is the gap between what you provide and what they customer already has available to them, either already purchased or offered by a competitor. You don't so much sell and market the USP itself but the incremental difference between yours and the competitors'.

This is the true value of what you have to offer. How do you reflect your true value through your website?

One interesting new development is the creation of multiple 'Microsites'. These sites may use the same delivery platform of hardware and software and will usually share some degree of corporate style but will offer users a different 'slice' through the organisation's information in a way that is much more targeted and focused.

Microsites could offer a slice through the corporate information either on a product by product basis or could be created to support a particular marketing campaign. In designing such a focused and targeted web presence there are a host of considerations to take a user friendliness is key. The aim is to provide a customer experience which envelopes and entices the user into performing a defined action or behaviour (transaction, click, etc.) This is ultimately the conversion point in the customer journey.

The film industry was one of the first users of the microsite method with each new film being provided with its own specific site (many of which are extremely comprehensive). The core reasons behind this innovation are twofold: To provide users an easy navigation to the relevant content (users want information on Harry Potter rather than on Warner Brothers), and; To allow site owners to subdivide and separate users and traffic based on either specific marketing campaigns or products.

For those organisations seeking to sell products and services through the web there are general rules to apply to ensure success. The 'shop front' is vitally important and must clearly enable product selection. The ordering process and fulfilment of the order must be a seamless flow of information both through the organisation and also through an updating response process to keep the customer advised of their order tracking.

Secure payment facilities are now widely available, accepting e-cash and credit and debit cards in a fully secure platform, many offering payment guarantees. PayPal is an aggregator taking away many of the complexities of setting up such processes and facilities yourself. iZettle a good example of a real world, cloud-based card processing product and service ideal for small or remotely operating businesses with low levels of transactions.

Whichever process is selected, the contracts made at the point of purchase are still legally binding. This does however become more complex when dealing across country or continent boundaries where different legal practice may apply. Legal disclaimers are essential to protect both the buyer and seller and these must be highly visible at a point early in the transaction process.

When considering the contracts and terms of engagement, it is vital that companies protect their trademarks and register all URL domain names (web addresses) that are relevant to their master brand. As in traditional media, copyright exists on all original works and therefore the source of any third party material must be attributed by the company using it.

Increasingly, apps are used as a distribution method by ad networks such as Google's AdSense, by media sites such as Flickr, by video sites such as YouTube and by hundreds of other organisations, and due to their 'viral nature' are also proactively used by bloggers, social network users, auction sites and owners of personal web sites., benefiting from one big advantage of the technology which is that the consumer does not have to click through to a website thereby saving their valuable time.

Apps can be a useful extension to a brand, when included in a broader portfolio of internet outreach along with blogs, online video, public relations, and micro-sites; all ways to extend your reach online.

Marketing Intimacy in Mobile Apps

By carefully plotting your customers' journeys you'll find the optimum place in their engagement with you where a mobile app should fit. It could be at the awareness creation stage, through customer acquisition or maybe later in the development of loyalty and advocacy as you retain them. Whatever the reasons, wherever the fit there seems to be a mantra for creating the most intimate mobile apps:

1. *Keep it relevant.* Only create and deliver an app if the customer really wants and needs it
2. *Customisable.* They will want to shape what you offer so it fits into their lives and delivers real value on their terms
3. *Personalised.* Vital they feel it's designed for them rather than a generic vanilla flavour
4. *Fresh.* Update it constantly with great content and media, otherwise you might as well point them to your website
5. *Customer Journey.* It needs to fit in the customer experience and perform a clearly defined role
6. *Hub Style.* Why not use it as a central portal for engagement and marketing conversation if your customers agree
7. *Device Friendly.* It doesn't have to work with all devices but it needs to work with the ones that your customers use

8. Social. Your customers will want this to be a window to their networks and yours, in the palm of their hand

9. Compatible Offline. We don't always have great mobile coverage so ensure the customer has a choice of offline and online

10. Shareable. Advocacy is everything in intimate marketing.

So the question you must ask yourself on behalf of you and your customer. Will my mobile app really deliver marketing intimacy?

Working closely with apps is the concept of QR Codes which in themselves could stimulate engagement and advocacy.

With many technologies that have remained in the public domain for over a decade there comes a time when it is make or break or perhaps acceptance that they will always remain in the background or niche applications.

The QR code, arguably a more flexible brother or sister to the famous bar-code, just may be about to have its day with the advent of the next generation of social media.

Social Media 2.0 was all about online interaction. Conversations and debates, sharing and caring through social media platforms such as Facebook and LinkedIn, Twitter and YouTube. But as we move steadily towards web 3.0 and perhaps social media 3.0 we are likely to see an increased blurring of virtual and real worlds.

QR codes just might be one of the fuels that links real and virtual world. At minimal cost you can download an app like QRafter to create your own QR codes with web link, an email address, v-card or text message associated with them.

This type of mobile tagging coupled with location-specific social media may well open up great possibilities for the creative communicators and marketers to both push messages but importantly engage with like-minded others who become advocates as they collect and then pass on those messages to their social networks.

Perhaps QR is about to come of age.

Checklist : Digital hub

If you were to describe your website as a person, who would they be?

In a perfect world, what would you expect and want your website to be delivering in terms of value to your business?

What job description will you give your website? Determine exactly what you need it to do. Be very specific and set it smart (specific, measurable, achievable, realistic and time bound) goals.

Where is your website currently positioned in your customers' journey and is this appropriate?

What improvements will you make to your website today from your recent observations and learning?

7.2 DELIVER : WEBSITES : BLOGS AND PEOPLE

Blogging has become a tool of choice for many organisations seeking to share their true values and innovation with the world. The word 'blog' is derived from the concept of weblog.

The evolution of blogging dates from 2005. Originally it took the form of a personal oriented narrative with a reflective nature, akin to a diary, commenting or shedding insight to a situation, scenario or opinion.

The ease of use, flexibility and accessibility of communications fostered by the internet made the blog easy to share. As bloggers also function as key hubs within the communications model, duplexing as opinion leaders in some cases and opinion formers in others, they have often been at the centre of the world of the early adopter.

A classic example of the latter is the renowned Robert Scoble; an ex Microsoft employee. Blogs amalgamate the uniqueness and power of personal publishing, which can be intoxicating and engaging and harness the ability to influence and inform communities.

Although Justin Hall, a student in the USA in 1994, is considered the founder of personal blogging, when he started to blog commentaries about his web discoveries, it is Jorn Barger who coined the term 'weblog' in 1997, on his site which consisted of a collection of his eclectic articles and websites. Two years later, Peter Merholz shortened the term to blog for short.

A key word associated with blogs is 'traffic' and as a result some blogs feature advertising which may fund other ancillary activities, depending on the author or, they may reflect the concerns or important causes of the author.

Popular writers are able to offer a lot of traffic, which attracts advertisers. The secret for the marketer then becomes how to aggregate this traffic. The following are some sites that provide insight into how the advertising industry is engaging with this medium by acting as intermediaries or affiliates.

Digital Content is about You not Me

There are a few simple steps in the art of writing effective content online that turn a tweet or a blog about Me into an engagement or start of a conversation about You:

Step 1. Remember that content is a combination of words, images and video. What will your audience want to experience, read, see, hear and watch?

Step 2. Prioritise your audience. You can't write for everyone at the same time so focus on those people most likely to listen, to engage and ultimately to add value to your strategy.

Step 3. Using Post-its, describe your organisation, products and services in motivating and engaging words and short phrases and in a language that your highest priority audience will understand. This is your content pot.

Step 4. Build a Content Wheel, putting the words and phrases from step 3 into one of the three Rule of Thirds segments (Point, Personal, Promote) to balance what you'll say and when.

Step 5. Look at your Website. What will your priority audience search with? Use the terms from your content wheel to build motivating and SEO-rich copy. Keep it concise, avoid repetition and use 'You' instead of 'We' or 'I'.

Step 6. Signpost specific pages and content on your website using Twitter. Remember # to glue your tweets to other people's tweets on the same subject. This will enhance both profile but importantly, relevance.

Step 7. Point to your web content using e-Newsletters. Turn bland title/subject lines into engaging hooks using your content wheel. It's a News letter and news is about people.

Step 8. If you have a personal opinion on a subject use the content wheel to populate and build blogs that position you or your 'face of the organisation' as current, relevant, informed and leave the reader with a clear 'call to action'; what do you want them to do next.

Step 9. Without overtly using copy-and-paste, ensure Linkedin,

Facebook and other social networks utilise all of the above because great digital content works across all platforms.

As the old dichotomy between push and pull marketing recedes, the key ingredient in the equation now is to grab attention. This in part has been the drive of the new business models for social networks such as Facebook, YouTube whereby the number of users gives commercial value to the organisation or individual YouTuber or Vlogger.

Although blogs are of use to all industries, they have had significant repercussions for the media sector, most notably with radio and newspapers whose control over what is said, when and to whom, has reduced significantly in recent years with the rise of consumer reporting.

Being Authentic in Online Communications

There are some key principles in effective persuasion and negotiation and for anyone in a customer facing role : marketing, sales, business development, customer service, senior management, leadership : it is vital to understand the perspective of the other person.

Authenticity is the most important thing to consider before you begin to replicate the behaviours of successful others. Being authentic means taking a long hard look at yourself and being honest about your strengths and weaknesses. The old saying 'play to your strengths' was created for just this purpose. I learnt a lot about this from listening to the feedback of others and how the world sees me and of course if you can consistently and honestly demonstrate these things then by definition you will be more appealing to the person you are negotiating with or persuading.

Once you understand yourself you can begin to emulate successful others who are already top tier negotiators and persuaders.

Reciprocity - You get what you give. It has always been this way because people feel obligated to return favours that are given to them. There are many theories around this element of human behaviour and the most common saying is probably 'treat others as you would like to be treated yourself'. I would add to this the fact that you are both seeking a mutually beneficial outcome so the phrase could be reinvented as 'treat others as you would like to be treated yourself so that you help each other reach a mutually beneficial result'. Your action - think about a win-win in all of your interactions.

Scarcity - If something is less easy to access or simply there is less of it, then human nature dictates it becomes more desirable. In marketing terms we might call this our USP; our unique selling proposition which is the key thing you can only get from me. Your action - what is it about engaging with you that the other person can't get from anyone else.

Authority - Since the dawn of time, people have always looked up to experts to lead them. Knowing and demonstrating knowledge, insight and wisdom on a particular subject can give you authority. This is different to telling someone what to do. It is more about leadership and sharing wisdom than it is preaching and telling. Your action - what do you know now that you could learn more about so that you become expert and invaluable to others.

Liking - Price, product, place, promotion, all those elements of the marketing mix have no bearing on a sales negotiation if the other person doesn't like the individual. Authenticity comes into play here because most people can see through fake others and so finding mutual interests, sharing amusing story telling and being genuinely interested in the other person all feed into the mirror effect that helps others to like us. Your action - listen, really listen to people you communicate with and find common ground from which you can build you conversations.

Consistency - We all like a maverick who stands out and entertains us, but in the art of negotiation and persuasion this kind of behaviour is at the other end of the scale to a consistent, predictable and reliable behaviour that allows the other person to steadily form their impressions and build trust. If you constantly change the terms of engagement you are beginning your conversation for the first time each time and eventually the other person will lose patience and switch off. Your action - Decide on the most important elements in your negotiation (benefits, price, people, whatever it might be) and keep them consistent whilst you discuss less vital ingredients.

Social Advocacy - In negotiation and persuasion we are always *seeking to develop mutual faith and trust. Assuming you still want to engage with the other person your final tool in the armoury is to use your previous contacts, peers, colleagues, customers and others to advocate you on your behalf. Whist the other person would probably expect you to paint yourself in a good light, if others are also saying these things about you, then you are far more likely to be believed. Your action - Develop a suite of testimonials, references and case studies that you can share and if they are from people just like the person you are negotiation with or persuading, then so much the better.*

And remember, the most important ingredient in the art of negotiation and persuasion is to always be yourself. If you force it you fail. Be authentic, listen and care, and everyone is a winner.

The variety of blogs is constantly multiplying. Perhaps the most common and fast expanding is the vlog, which is a blog comprising videos. Others make extensive use of photographs, called a photoblog. Flickr, Instagram and Snapchat are rapidly expanding examples of the popularity and something that shouldn't be ignored by the savvy marketer.

The issue of authenticity is central to blogging. Marketers and brand managers have to be aware of maintaining credibility before visibility.

Fake or spoof blogs can do great damage to a company's reputation. A famous example of this was "Walmarting across America" in which two Walmart enthusiasts travelled across America reporting on their experiences as they visited Walmarts on their journey. Whilst the two people did do the journey it emerged that they had been paid to do it by Walmart.

Whilst it could be argued that due to demands on internal resources there is a case to outsource blogging to an agency.

However with the growing popularity of video blogging (vlogging) there is becoming nowhere to hide.

With the vlog the speaker/publisher is there on the screen for all to see and this is the power and reason why it is quickly becoming the most effective form of engagement in current content management.

A whole new industry of wealthy, professional vloggers has formed, reviewing products, sharing and documenting their lives and as a consequence becoming highly influential in the eyes and minds of their loyal fan bases.

This has a significant importance for businesses and their marketers because there is now a proven and well documented methodology for best practice vlogging which can be applied by organisations seeking to cut through the competitive noise.

Business vloggers such as Gary Vaynerchuk and Tony Robbins are good examples of successful business people who have turned to vlogging to supplement and compliment their commercial activities, sharing advice, tips and guidance as well as documenting the process.

The momentum that this vlogging documentation creates is impressive in the groundswell both of followers but also positive commercial energy and spin-off networking opportunities that can in turn be monetised by the vloggers and their corporations behind them.

If documentation of internal processes and day to day activities is a step too far for your strategy at this time, consider what regular content you could create and distribute through video channels that would stimulate engagement as part of your content strategy.

Vlogging for business development is still in relative infancy and as such the early pioneers using the skills and experience of the celebrity YouTubers in a business sense are beginning to disrupt the traditional digital marketing model.

Checklist : Blogs and people

Do you currently have a blog and is it performing a strong and evidenced ROI?

In an ideal world, who in your organisation could or should be blogging as the face of the business and relevant in the customers' eyes?

Do you have the writing expertise and ambition inside the business or is blogging an activity to outsource to a third party?

How will blogging, perhaps as a form of thought leadership or documentation, support your higher level content strategy?

What will you change or include today in your blogging (or vlogging) to enhance your customer engagement?

7.3 DELIVER : WEBSITES : CUSTOMER AND SEARCH OPTIMISATION

Social Advocacy Strategy

Social Media Advocacy has been been at the heart of the most successful social networkers' plans for a number of years, but now it should be at the core of everyone's online strategy.

You have Facebook, Twitter, Linkedin and Google+ accounts and you spend lots of your time posting updates, watching what others post and sometimes contributing to message threads in shared groups and fora. You feel busy because you are publishing, sharing and contributing.

You have been measuring the success of your activities by watching your growing number of Likes, Followers and Connections. As the numbers grow you feel satisfied you must be getting good value from the time and energy you are committing.

The good news is that you are probably seeing some value and if you are keeping people engaged online then you are creating a great platform for generating new business opportunities from them.

However one big test of just how good your networks are is whether or not your connections, friends and followers are advocates.

Advocates are defined as connections who share your communications on your behalf with their networks. They regularly re-tweet, they click 'share' and they distribute your content far and wide.

In simple terms they are marketing your business for you and the intrinsic quality of each piece of advocated content is up to 10 times the value of anything that you could publish yourself. Social advocacy is the equivalent of a digital recommendation and as we know word-of-mouth can be one of the most powerful marketing tools in your armoury.

So the next time you publish some content, engage in a

discussion thread, or make a new connection, think:
1. Is this something that is easily sharable?
2. Have I written to provide value for my contacts' contacts or just my first tier of connections?
3. Did I really think about publishing the right content in the right place at the right time to help my advocates advocate?
4. Can I measure the reach of everything I publish to test just how far and wide the message went?
5. Will I remember to thank each and every advocate for the time they took to share my content?

If you can answer yes to each of these five points then you do have a social advocacy strategy. If you can't then you now know where to begin.

Long Tail Content

There are different stages in customer engagement that will make SEO more or less relevant at different points. This idea is called Customer Optimisation and is actually as important as SEO in terms of the actual experience the customer enjoys after the SEO has worked and brought them to the website.

Different things will apply to their experience depending on where they are in their customer journey:

Awareness stage – reaching customers who would otherwise not be aware of the organisation, its brands, products and services

Conversion stage – turning this awareness into the buying process and converting them from aware prospects into customers

Retention stage – ensuring existing customers are not just old customers but actively up-buying and cross-buying and behaving as loyal advocates.

Optimisation must ensure it addresses all three stages for the benefit of the search engine and also the customer experience.

A key method of achieving this is called Long Tail Content. Long Tail Search Phrases are one of the key search ranking criteria that Google and the other dominant search engines have been using for many years to rate your site against the competition.

Long Tail is vital to search engine optimisation because it equates a specific reference to a page for the search engine spiders and robots.

Specificity is the key ingredient. The longer the search phrase the fewer people will search using it but those who do will be perfectly targeted towards the appropriate page on your website. The search engines are equating the value of 100 people coming to your web page and it being relevant to the financial value of that visit to you. They would rank lower a search optimised page that is less specific and generates 100,000 people but for whom the actual experience on the page is irrelevant.

Social Business : Have you got the SPIEL?

It's all about SPIEL. Strategise, Provoke, Inform, Engage, Learn.

Strategise - Don't just 'do social' if either your business or your customer isn't ready for it. Some industries are still quite nicely running with the traditional, old school marketing model of the 7Ps in the marketing mix, thank you very much. Some customer segments aren't considered to be fully embracing social media and are readily discounted. But are you sure? Really sure? Don't fall into the trap of thinking that your customers are all of a slightly more advanced age profile and unable to switch on a computer. Do the research and don't make assumptions, then build medium term strategies (nobody can forecast accurately how this will change beyond say three years hence), to gain competitive advantage.

Provoke - Push your business to commit to being a social business. It's not enough to show up and develop a great online platform, website and social networking accounts and then go back to doing business the old way. Social businesses live and breathe constant engagement, on the customers' terms, through their chosen media, when and where they want to do it. If you still think marketing is about old fashioned 'push' of messages and advertising then your competitors are already one step ahead of you.

Inform - Here's the real deal. It's all about getting the conversation started and that's the role of the social business marketer. Have great content ready. When you blog it's about starting the conversation not just telling stories about the world according to you. Share experience, knowledge, information and news. Add value using phrases that your customers are likely to use when they search for the kinds of things your are able to offer them. Remember it is two way traffic so always end your information with a question mark. Invite response.

Engage - Your entire business should be helping with the ongoing engagement with target customers and prospects. Engagement means social conversation. Not tucked away deep in an email thread but in public, on social networks for all to see. Yes, good and bad things. Compliments and complaints. Embrace all engagement as a chance to develop that vital customer intimacy because that's the fuel for the all important advocacy at the end of their customer journey.

Learn - You won't be a social business overnight. It takes time, resource, commitment and endeavour to sustain your early momentum. Learn who in your organisation can support you to make it happen and what it really is that makes your customers full engaged. In social business it's the art of listening as much as it is the art of talking.

In long tail content and long tail search, less is more, as it equates to a higher value per visitor.

The trick is in the tail, those key words that your ideal customers would use to find you, your products and your services.

Imagine you are a hotel in Cornwall providing high quality family accommodation and activities. You know your ideal customer. On your website you start to write for them, about them, in their language and on their terms. You do not bombard the search engines with generic terms like 'hotel' or 'B&B' or 'discount breaks'. Leave that to the competition, to fight over woolly search words that could apply equally to a backpacker searching for accommodation in Australia as they could a retired couple in Canada seeking a weekend away.

The search savvy marketer is now thinking specifically about exactly what words and phrases their ideal persona/customer would use when describing their hotel. Phrases such as 'family friendly hotel in Cornwall' or 'activity breaks in Cornwall for families'. These have long tails. They mean something for the target customer, they are relevant to the hotel itself and importantly they are search engine friendly and help you to both rise in the search engine result pages as well as provide that 'relevance' link for when people actually arrive at the hotel's website.

And how do you measure that you are getting better at using your long tail rather than short tail? It is in your 'bounce rate'. That is the measure of how many people are arriving at your website only to see that it is not quite what they wanted or searched for. They simply bounce off without visiting pages deeper in your site. Lower bounce rates from using your long tail strategy will show you an early indication that you are on the right tracks. From there you can really start to measure the customer experience in the digital journey you give them.

Checklist : Customer and search engine optimisation

Is your website search engine optimised for all long tail phrases that your target customer will search on?

Have you tested your website content with Google search tools for improved optimisation?

What additional pages and site content can you add or improve today to attract more of your target persona to your website?

Once your target customer persona has arrived at the appropriate landing page, is their experience optimal to take them to their next step in their customer journey?

From your target customers' perspective, what improvements can you make today to their website journey, to showcase your use of the Rule of Thirds and to ensure there are an appropriate number of steps to consolidate their faith and trust in your business?

8.1 DELIVER : SOCIAL MEDIA : FROM REACTIVE TO PROACTIVE

As we reflect on our choices of social networks to populate our customer personas' journeys we must ensure we focus on those in which they are already present and active.

This knowledge will ensure that we can focus our time and energy in the right networks for the right reasons.

If a social network is clearly positioned in the customer journey for a particular purpose (increase awareness, help convert the awareness into a purchase or commitment, or in the retention phase) then we describe it as proactive. In other words we'll be using it proactively in our marketing strategy.

The converse is a social network which isn't directly relevant to the target customer persona and will not be assigned a position in the customer journey. We won't be using it proactively and in other words we will have an account set up for each but they will be reactively updated with content to keep them live, even though they don't have a specific job description.

Having reactive social networks is important for search engine optimisation and especially in your relationship with Google. For example, as part of the Google family, you should set up and ensure you have reactive YouTube and Google+ accounts even if they don't form part of the customer journey.

The Best Time for Social Networking

They say in comedy that timing is everything and it appears for successful social networking the same is very true. Back in the dawn of web 2.0 (social media, to you and me) if you were actively posting about what you were up to and your thoughts on every subject under the sun then all was well and you thought of yourself as a digitally social being.

Those days have long since passed and the word on digital street now is that less is most definitely more. With the background noise on social networks reaching unprecedented levels you could be mistaken for thinking you have to be omnipresent and trying to shout louder than the next digital extrovert. But this isn't actually true.

The art of effective social networking is now about cutting through the noise with carefully worded and carefully timed communication. Notice that I didn't just say 'tweets' and I didn't say 'status updates'. It's more than this. Social networking is now about words, images and video. The full mix of media.

We are simply talking about timing. Whatever your choice of media or social network there will be certain times of the day and days of the week when your target connections, friends, peers and followers are awake and ready to engage. You need to find this optimum time. Or it could be times, because there will probably be some peaks and troughs as you look through the statistics of your social week.

So where do these helpful statistics hide? Well there are numerous digital dashboards, each claiming to be more comprehensive than the next. Some are complex and some are very simple.

As a starting point I use SocialReport.com Simple login process, easy to set up and does what it says on the tin. The best bit is that not only will it provide a snapshot of evidence of the peaks and troughs of when your audience should be most receptive but it also gives you a glimpse of their collective interests and hobbies. When we say to engage emotionally as well as professionally, what better balance to strike than to fire up a conversation or signpost a link to their collective passions.

Do your research, work out your best timing and then set to work to provide quality engagement through social media. And if you find that the ideal time is inconvenient to you then you can always use something like Hootsuite to schedule in some automated social media posting, just to get the conversations started.

Checklist : From reactive to proactive

What job descriptions will you give to each of your social networks, based on the value you want them to deliver both to your business goals and your customers' experience?

Which social networks will be proactive (part of a customer persona's journey) and what role are they playing and at which point in the journey?

Which social networks will be reactive and solely created for the purposes of search engine optimisation and blocking out competitors from taking search engine result places?

What improvements, changes and tuning of your social media will you make today and how and when will you measure the effects?

8.2 DELIVER : SOCIAL MEDIA : SOCIAL MEDIA GUIDELINES

Marketers typically focus on positives and position their offering in terms of benefits and great outcomes for the customer. This has always been the case.

However we must ensure that customer concerns are also addressed, to give a balanced, considered, pragmatic and realistic view.

Customers will be concerned about the security of their engagement and sharing of personal information. GDPR regulations in Europe go some way to addressing these concerns.

They are also concerned about lack of control where the balance in the relationship swings to the organisation when the customer gives their personal details, credit card information and preferences.

Superfluous data collection both contravenes the data regulations and increases customer suspicions that the privacy and security of their information is being compromised. To allay these fears marketers should declare openly how the customers' information will be held and used and the reasons for retaining it. If the customer deems the reasons worthy they will be confident in the brand and their side of the relationship.

This level of consideration is at the heart of successful customer relationship management and marketing information system management, to the benefit of both customer and marketer.

Digital marketers must ensure they are familiar with and compliant with relevant legislation and of course any specific regulation in their industry.

In particular, marketers should become familiar with the key provisions of each of the following:

Advertising Standards Authority (ASA), Committee of Advertising Practice Code (CAP) 2011

Distance Selling Regulations (DSR)
Electronic Commerce (EC Directive) Regulations 2002 (ECR)
Provision of Service Regulations 2009
Misleading Marketing Regulations 2008
Privacy and Electronic Communications Regulations (Cookie Law)
General Data Protection Regulation (GDPR) 2018

CAP Code, enforced by the Advertising Standards Authority (ASA) Since 1 March 2011, the non-broadcast Committee of Advertising Practice (CAP) Code has been extended to include marketing messages on businesses own websites, and other online content under their control.

This means that both paid-for and non-paid-for advertising and marketing online must now comply with the CAP Code. This includes: banner and commercial classified adverts - including adverts within emails; pop-up adverts; paid-for search listings; paid-for listings on price comparison sites; statements on your website intended to sell or promote your product or service; sales and marketing messages on social networking pages under your control, for example Facebook or Twitter; paid-for and non-paid-for sales promotions.

However, the extended scope of the CAP Code does not include user-generated content on your website, or similar feedback on social networking sites, unless you incorporate it into your own marketing material.

The Distance Selling Regulations (DSR) and Electronic Commerce (EC Directive) Regulations 2002 (ECR) may apply if you are selling goods without a face-to-face interaction on the internet, by email or text messaging.

If you are not selling physical goods but are selling services, then the Provision of Services Regulations 2009 apply instead.

If you are not trading to consumers but are purely business to business, then you need to check the Business Protection from Misleading Marketing Regulations 2008. This is particularly important if you are publishing comparisons of your products against competitors.

The Privacy and Electronic Communications Regulations

(PECR) is the so called 'Cookie Law' but it also covers all electronic marketing communications including email, text, picture and video marketing messages.

If you know the name of the person you are sending your electronic communication to, then it is the General Data Protection Regulations (GDPR) that are one of the most important sets of rules that all businesses must comply with both online and offline if there is any form of storing of prospect or customer information.

Under the GDPR it is not sufficient to be compliant, there is also an obligation to be able to "demonstrate" that compliance. For example the GDPR requires organisations to carry out a privacy impact assessment (PIA) before carrying out "high risk" processing. Examples of high risk processing include using a new technology, or processing sensitive information on a large scale (such as information about health, ethnic background and so on). The PIA should describe what you plan to do, an assessment of the necessity and proportionality, an assessment of the risks, and the measures that will be put in place to address those risks. Even if the obligation to carry out a formal PIA has not been triggered then the organisation will still need to assess the data protection risks and take appropriate measures to protect personal data.

Some organisations will also be required to appoint a GDPR Officer who must be independent from senior management.

Another area where the accountability principle may bite is around consent. If for example, you obtain consent for sending marketing mailshots then you should record who consented, when, what words were used to obtain consent (eg, a copy of the consent form) plus how they consented (eg, through your website or at an event they attended).

Getting the accountability principles wrong could have serious implications. A worst case scenario would be a fine or having to pay compensation to affected individuals. The maximum fines are going to be increased from the current £500,000 to the higher of €20 million or 4% of worldwide turnover.

Core to the directives are the reasonable protection of members of the public and as such permission-based digital marketing should be at the centre of digital plans.

Organisations must research the needs and desires of their target audience and if appropriate various segments. Communications should be personalised and relevant wherever possible and have something new to say each time. Importantly from October 2003 an EU directive stated that prior to sending unsolicited email or SMS a specific and explicit 'opt-in' must have been received from the proposed recipient.

In the USA an opt out law is proposed and this may legitimise spam (which currently makes up an estimated 80% of all email traffic). Persistently offending organisations that do not comply with this legislation can be referred to ICSTIS and individuals may register with the telephone preference service (TPS) to cover opt-out of all such contact.

For more information: visit http://www.dma.org.uk

Checklist : Guidelines

What policies and guidelines do you have in place to ensure consistency of your social media usage by all involved?

From what you have learned, what changes and improvements will you make to your digital marketing guidelines?

Are you compliant with legislation and regulations specific to your industry?

How will you stay up to date with legislation, regulations and best practice?

What improvements will you make today to your social media and digital marketing guidelines?

8.3 DELIVER : SOCIAL MEDIA : TWITTER, FACEBOOK, LINKEDIN, ET AL

Whilst the descriptions of 'how to' set-up and utilise each of the social networks is beyond the scope of this book, it's important to highlight the main purposes of each and how they might contribute value at specific points in the customer journey, or as we have seen, remain as reactive tools in our digital marketing mix.

The example positions in the customer journey are considerations rather than absolutes or recommendations, because each customer journey and its related tactical decisions is specific to each brand and organisation. However, we see some typical examples such as:

Instagram - An image-focused network gaining quickly in popularity and usage. Often used to geographically target users # tagging subjects and locations in real-time. Strong search facility means it's particularly helpful in the awareness phase of the customer journey.

Pinterest - Useful for pinning all images on your website to aid search engine optimisation with each pin being an incremental inbound link to your site. Possibly a reactive tool rather than directly positioned in the customer journey.

Facebook - Ubiquitous site with arguably the most targeted advertising tool available, allowing personas to be replicated and exclusively targeted by a step by step profiling tool. Because of its flexibility and multitude of uses from a blogging platform to online forum it is helpful in any position in the customer journey. Russian equivalent is VK.

Google+ - Lesser used social network in real terms, but vital to maintain as part of the Google family of services (also including YouTube, Gmail, Google Analytics). Likely to be a reactive tool rather than used in the customer journey, unless the persona is already active in Google+

YouTube - The world's most popular video network and part of the Google family. A useful tool in the customer journey in the awareness phase just before the conversion point. It and also be used to serve the customer in there retention phase with 'how to' guides and 'frequently answered questions' to aid product or service usage.

Linkedin - A popular business network with equivalents in Germany (XING) and France (Viadeo). Very strong search filters and 'big data' capability, especially for business to business marketers.

Snapchat - Fast moving social network with images, videos and a proliferation of emojis. Unlike most social networks where content posted remains in a legacy timeline, Snapchat is more focused on immediacy and real-time communication and most content posted automatically deletes itself within days or upon viewing.

At the core of all the social networks is the concept for the marketer of word of mouth marketing (WOM) which refers to any interpersonal communications which the receiver views as impartial. In essence it is as simple as a colleague coming into work and telling the team that the film they saw last night was excellent and well worth going to see.

WOM can be positive or negative and therefore the challenge for the marketer is twofold. Firstly how best to manage and capitalise on positive WOM and how to minimise negative WOM. For the latter good product quality/satisfaction of promised benefits and good customer
service are essential.

Since their inception, social networking websites, such as Facebook, have attracted millions of users, many of whom have integrated these sites into their daily routines.

Social networking websites have been defined as "web-based services that allow individuals to construct a public or semi-public profile within a bounded system, articulate a list of other users with whom they share a connection, and view and traverse their list of connections and those made by others within the system. The nature and nomenclature of these connections may vary from site to site."

What makes social networking sites unique to marketers are that they contain engaged people who are communicating in their own space and place. They perceive that they own it.

Business to business social networking sites like LinkedIn encourage the extension of a social network in the true sense of by promoting the 'networking' element for knowledge sharing, discussion, research and career progression.

Most social networking profiles consist of contacts, friends or followers, who themselves are members of the same network. Most sites encourage their members to create media rich personal profiles through which they can be easily found and connected to by their real world friends, peers, contacts and business associates.

Social networks predominantly focus on one form of media content as their lead tool for information sharing.

Text - LinkedIn, WhatsApp, Twitter (although arguably images)
Images - Instagram, Pinterest, Snapchat, Facebook (although arguably video)
Video - YouTube, Vimeo

Social media marketing allows businesses and websites to gain popularity, engagement and advocacy.

There are five distinct advantages to social media marketing that make it a vital tool to any
marketing campaign including:

1. Better targeting – social media marketing can draw a highly targeted segment of internet users to visit a business or website, increasing visibility of content on both a local and global level
2. High return on investment – social networking is one of the most cost effective methods of marketing, providing a high return on investment. Low investment means low risk to even the smallest business
3. Does not require specialist technical skills – most social networking sites are visually oriented and straightforward, which means that all marketers can use social networking tools
4. Works better than online adverts campaigns – because most internet users are bombarded with adverts every day, as a whole, society has become so used to them people are starting to become less receptive to them. Social media marketing provides a personalised view point to attract potential customers to the things

that interest them in a space and at a time that suits them

Social Network Marketing has revolutionised the way organisations can communicate to their customers and extends the tools available to carry out relationship marketing along the customer journey.

Organisations that are engaging with social network marketing tools have been labelled as networked enterprises, or social businesses. These organisations are expertly implementing this exercise into wider customer relationship strategies and are experiencing growth and reward for their time and investment as a result.

This focus on the customer involves in-depth research and constant listening and re-evaluation of every aspect of social networking campaigns and activities. Research and evaluation form the very essence of the social media marketing process.

Traditional marketing techniques can still be applied in social media marketing. The planning process should still address the elements of the 'marketing mix' or the 'Seven Ps' and there may be some more 'Ps' involved when discussing social network planning:

- Publics – refers to both the external and internal stakeholders, which might include the target audience, secondary audiences, policymakers, gatekeepers and influencers, those who are involved in some way with either approval or implementation of a product/service
- Partnership – with other organisations in the community you work in who share similar goals to yours identifying ways you can work together
- Policy – social marketing can be effective at changing public perceptions and behaviours, but is difficult to sustain unless the environment supports that change long term. Media advocacy programs can be an effective complement to a social marketing campaign

 Purse – how will the social networking be paid for

The benefits to marketers in utilising effective social media marketing are that it can:
- Increase knowledge
- Influence attitudes

- Show benefits of behaviour change
- Reinforce knowledge, attitudes, and behaviour
- Demonstrate skills
- Prompt an immediate action
- Increase demand for services
- Refute myths and misconceptions

Influence norms
Give prospects the confidence to convert to customers

Social networking tools are used by marketers to help build stronger and deeper relationships, but only if brands identify which platforms work best for them and concentrate their efforts. "If you're a small company dealing in products which aren't engaging, like concrete or electrical components, to devote a huge amount of your marketing budget to Facebook would be a mistake, as the volume of people interested will be minimal. Whereas a viral campaign can increase mentions of a 'less sexy' brand across these channels," says Christian Howes, Head of Solutions Engineering at digital agency Webtrends.

The art of good digital marketing has always been based on a deep understanding of target customers and their behaviours. Facebook profiling within business to business or business to consumer campaigns allows a highly specific and targeted range of data to be integrated into advertising for maximum value from pay per click and pay per impression.

The power of this opportunity to connect with the consumer cannot be overemphasised for a marketer. Social networking allows multiple connection points between almost anyone on the planet. Information about an organisation can be found, shared, enjoyed, debated, criticised and tracked by anybody who cares to be interested. As any endorsements are established and cross-referenced, the profile of an organisation, a product or a service can grow exponentially as more and more people become exposed to and share a marketing message.

Immediacy in Digital Marketing

There is a phrase in marketing communications and advertising called the 'call to action'.

At the point in watching an advert, opening some direct mail or engaging in social media there is a moment at which the marketer believes that the customer has just enough information and confidence to take their next step in the customer journey. Sometimes this is as simple as a 'click here for more information'. At other times it might be a 'call us on this number to buy'.

Now there is a new and improved version of the call to action and it's the Immediate Call To Action.

Immediacy is something as consumers we have become familiar with. No longer are we happy to wait 48 hours to receive a reply to our enquiry. If we email we sit and wait for a reply within minutes and anything much longer and we are on the phone to chase it up. Immediacy is commonplace. Instant gratification is the name of the game but it's not one way traffic.

Online retailer The Hut Group took things back to the customer with immediate effect through their iwantoneofthose.com store. Yes there are the motivating price discounts, 2 for £20 and free delivery offers but the best yet, in line with that 'press the button right here, right now' ethos is the following:
- 20% off everything but not for long
- Discount reduced by 1% on the hour every hour
- Enter code TICKTOCK
- BUY NOW

So here's why this approach is genius
- A healthy discount % from the recommended retail price inspires interest in the products for sale
- If a customer pauses to purchase then the longer they pause the less the benefit to them
- The code is highlighted in capitals which in digital world is the equivalent of shouting
- The button to press to BUY NOW is prominent, ensuring the next step in the customer journey is clear

Such a simple tactic matches customer behaviour to marketer's need.

So think today about how easy and motivating you could make your purchase decision point. Are you truly stimulating customers to buy right here, right now?

Checklist : Twitter, Facebook, Linkedin, Instagram and YouTube

Are you aware of current best practice in creating, managing and using each of the social networks relevant to your target persona?

How will you keep your skills and knowledge of the key social networks up to date and fresh?

How does your performance in each social network compare to that of your most important competitors?

What changes and improvements will you make today to each social network based on your learning and experience?

9.1 DELIVER : CAMPAIGNS : PAID, OWNED, EARNED MEDIA

The purpose of a digital marketing campaign is to encourage and facilitate a pre-defined behaviour.

This behaviour is likely to be defined in the Conversion point of the customers' journey. It might be a product or service sale, the signing of a contract, or another pre-defined action whereby a prospect converts into a customer.

The campaign, even though it may be defined as a digital marketing campaign, is likely to also have a blend of offline tools and moments where the target customer experiences things in the real world as well as through their screen.

As we have already established, the customer journey, and in this instance the campaign, must consider every step of engagement from the very first time they encounter the start of the campaign, through to and ongoing retention and continued engagement post-purchase.

The RACE Framework of Reach, Act, Convert, Engage is a very useful checklist to begin the construction of the campaign flow, developed by Smart Insights.

Reach - establish which social networks and publishing tools you will need to include in your campaign to draw the target customer into the content hub. The target customer is exploring and considering their options.

Act - decide the hub (possibly within your website) where you will direct your target customers their journey. The customer is making their decision at this point.

Convert - the conversion point, likely to be the point of purchase, is where the customer needs to have established trust in your brand and what they are purchasing. The extended digital marketing mix (see section 5.3) will come into play at this point in their journey.

Engage - post-purchase, where the prospect has now become

a customer, is when and through which digital marketing tools, to help stimulate advocacy (sharing of their great experience with their peers, colleagues, family and friends).

Measurement in all its forms is covered later in the book and relies on a clear timeline, focus on specific marketing tools, integrated into a seamless, end-to-end customer journey for each target customer persona.

The journey is fuelled with relevant content at each step and that content should be appropriate for where the customer is in their journey. At the Awareness stage they will need more informative content to educate them as to the value of the brand, products and services and to help them build faith in the offer. At the Conversion stage it's all about trust. In the Retention phase all of these subjects will have been covered so it is about helping the customer confirm for themselves they have made the right decision, stimulating loyalty and encouraging advocacy.

Digital Marketing is an Investment Not a Cost in Campaigns, Events and Launches

In many organisations the spend on marketing activities is perceived as a cost.
Different departments, board directors and even marketers themselves invariably consider marketing spend as a budget. By definition a budget is an amount of money dedicated for spending on items and activity. And therefore it follows that such spend is a cost and the word cost has negative connotations.

Most businesses, and especially those who don't have effective marketing planning processes, allocate a set amount of budget to marketing with the vague notion that it will be spent on some kind of activity that will assist business growth. Such activity tends to be sporadic, unplanned, disjointed and sometimes chaotic. It's understandable though. By giving someone, even a seasoned marketing professional, a pot of money and asking them to spend it, can cloud judgment and put the individual under undue pressure to spend even if there is actual need to spend. The larger the organisation and the more widely spread the budget across various business units and countries and the pressures and chaos increase.

So here's a thought. Forget marketing budget as a cost and think of marketing activities as an investment. Rather then simply allocating a random amount (how often do you hear words like, "you had that amount of budget last year and this year you are fortunate because we are going to increase it by 10%" or "this year we will be cutting your budget by 10%, but we want you to do more this year".) and then looking for ways to spend it, how about starting with a marketing budget of zero.

Yes I said it. You have a marketing budget of zero.

Now the fun begins because you have to work out ways of creating marketing activities that will add real value to your business. Please read that again... REAL VALUE TO YOUR BUSINESS.

As we have seen, marketing budget is a cost because it is a sum of money that the business would actually rather take as a dividend payment or reinvest back into the business. So your task if you accept zero marketing budget is to propose strategic and tactical activities that each will deliver a return to the business.

You begin of course with all the favourite marketing planning exercises and out of that will come a wish list of activities that will create and sustain excellent value for the customer at the same time as delivering business development, sales opportunities and customer service support. There will be new product development opportunities and often the chance to enter a new market or diversify. Whatever the outputs of your planning each and every proposed activity must be shown to deliver a tangible value back to the business. I emphasise a TANGIBLE value.

The value may be in increased revenue, additional sales volumes, strategic partnerships or simply more effective ways of working leading to efficiency savings.

If you place a value against every activity and of course a way of measuring and reporting that value then the allocation of spend (I am not using the word budget here) against that activity can be shown to deliver an incremental gain. Spend a dollar and return five dollars. Invest a pound in an activity and return ten pounds in value to the business.

Whatever the outcome for each element of spend you undertake, the importance is that you will have turned around the way the business views marketing. Perform your marketing role in this way and you will be seen as adding strategic and short term value rather than simply being 'that person who spends money, and we aren't sure quite what they do'.

Following the rules, written or unwritten. Listening to the 'best practice' spouted by consultants, the media and your Facebook friends. Often it's just the same thing, re-presented in a slightly different way.

And herein lies your opportunity. It's called Disruptive Marketing (definition: "A disruptive innovation is an innovation that helps create a new market and value network, and eventually disrupts an existing market and value network (over a few years or decades), displacing an earlier technology. The term is used in business and technology literature to describe innovations that improve a product or service in ways that the market does not expect, typically first by designing for a different set of consumers in a new market and later by lowering prices in the existing market." source: Wikipedia).

By taking a completely different look at your market, your customers, your products, the technologies that help you to do business, your systems and processes and your people... dare to dream. Take time out and think "what if...". Try not to be bound by the past but think of an ideal future. Don't be constrained by following the same old tracks. Yes stop, look and listen, but not to reinvent an iteration of the existing, but rather to sense something new, something that will fundamentally change for the better, a feature of your marketplace.

The key to successful digital advertising is they ability to bring sound and movement to a traditionally one-dimensional media.

With the decrease in attention spans of 21st century target audiences, coupled with their unwillingness to read off screen for more than an average 400 word count, digital advertising presents brands with an effective way to engage and resonate with target audiences by presenting a fusion of sound, movement, entertainment, insight and information.

Digital advertising also allows digital newspapers to offer a multi-media experience to their reader who will often see a 'still' of an advert in the digital paper and by clicking on the picture bring the ad 'to life' as a visual and audio production.

Online advertising is now big business and numerous tools exist for tracking individual users through to general site traffic statistics showing numbers of click-throughs from a particular online advertisement. Having attracted a visitor to an organisations website they then need to be either influenced, educated, or sold to.

For organisations seeking to sell a product or service through the web there are general rules to apply to ensure success. The 'shop front' is vitally important and must clearly enable product selection. The ordering process and fulfilment of the order must be a seamless flow of information both through the organisation and also through an updating response process to keep the customer advised of their order tracking.

One of the quickest and flexible means to capture traffic to websites is Pay Per Click (PPC) advertising.

PPC, as the name suggests, are adverts placed on other websites (or potentially emails) that direct users to your website. Google's Adwords is the most well known PPC service though all search engines and social networks provide a similar service. In social networks, individual posts or tweets can be 'boosted' to increase the reach of the message and potentially attract more clicks by visitors.

The essentials of PPC are:
• The company selects the key words, phrases that they believe users will use within their searches or the posts/tweets most likely to be engaged with
• They create an advert (text or graphic) that is designed to attract the user.
• The company decides how much each click on the advert is worth and sets a maximum CPC (cost per click) or a defined maximum budget and leaves the distribution and timing of the ad to the service provider.
• The advert distributor (e.g. Google) places these adverts on pages either in their search engine (Search Ads) or on the websites of content providers who subscribe (Content Ads).
• Usually multiple adverts will be placed with the position and ranking defined by the amount the company is willing to pay (Pay

more and get a better position on the page).
- If a visitor clicks on the advert they are directed to the company's website and the company pays the distributor (e.g. Google). If the ad is on a content page then the distributor will split the revenue with the content provider.
- An advertiser may bid and 'buy up' certain key words or phrases relevant to their product or service, with the price they have to pay depending on the demand for the word. This is known as
Cost per Click (CPC).

If search and display advertising are tracked together, then the advertiser and agency, if they use one, can really understand their customer's path to conversion. For example, a visitor engages with an advert for the first time. Then three days later they use a search engine to look for the product name they remembered seeing on the advert. They click on the PPC sponsorship link but do not go through to purchase. Finally, on day eight they convert via a different ad on a different publisher, making a purchase on the advertiser's website.

Traditionally, the conversion would only be awarded to the last ad or keyword seen. But when the whole path is analysed, we see the value of each touch point along the path. The trends of each of the channels and publishers that drive the conversions can be shown, and their individual media attribution values calculated and this re-marketing enables marketers to plan their budgets better across search and display in order to achieve the best return on investment.

Affiliate Marketing

Affiliate marketing is an arrangement through which an online retailer pays commission to an external website for visitors or sales that are generated from its referrals. In essence it is collaboration between busy website owners.

Intermediary sites, as the term suggests, are sites that offer elements of both end points and launchpads. They may contain significant content and will seek to attract users and returning users but will mainly earn their revenue from users leaving via paid for links.

Blogs are a classic intermediary and affiliate sites but shopping comparison sites also act as intermediary sites and are one of the fastest developing areas of the internet and are approaching saturation in some market sectors. These sites will pay for inbound traffic and aim to earn more money from outbound traffic, either via PPC advertising or referral fees from sites such as Amazon. These sites expect a dwell time somewhere between those of an End Point site and a Launchpad site.

Customer paths through the website may be lengthy or very short. In general a short customer path tends to result in a relatively generic exit point (earning the site owner lower income) whereas a longer path (for example in a comparison site) will tend to provide a higher quality (and thus higher earning) exit point.

Regular re-visitors to blog websites where there are very high levels of subscribers can also lead to attractive affiliate marketing arrangements.

It is common for search engine companies, such as Yahoo for example, to be paid a fee (usually a one off or yearly subscription) by a company or individual in order to be included in their index. The rationale is to maintain credibility amongst website users in order for them not to be exposed to multifarious adverts. Blogging sites with high volumes of traffic have again championed this technique.

Advertising is a non-personal form of communication targeted at a large but defined audience and is ideal, in conjunction with Rule of Thirds content and Word of Mouth, at the Awareness phase of the customer's journey.

Advertising is intended to attract the customers' attention and interest. Specific objectives might include: to raise awareness, increase sales, inform, counter competition, reassure, remind, or to support personal selling.

Sell Outcomes

Content Strategy is as much about careful planning as it is being spontaneous and exciting in the things you communicate.

The key to successful content is always to evoke an emotional response from your target audience and especially your target Persona.

There are always so many distractions and reasons why your Personas will be bombarded with enticing messages and communications from your competitors. There will be special offers, incentives and discounts. There will be new product launches and great case studies and testimonials from others just like them. All of this is designed to pique the interest of your Persona; to cut through the noise.

However your Persona is savvy and has seen and heard all of these things before. They will have seen countless businesses who claim to be professional with the highest levels of service. They'll have endured numerous claims that push all manner of wares and in time your Persona gets tired and switches off.

Your biggest challenge with your Content Strategy is to emotionally engage your Persona. Forget the features and benefits of your products and services. Everyone says pretty much the same thing. Begin with how you feel. Share emotionally charged messages that demonstrate you are real people, marketing and selling real things, that you enjoy yourselves.

A great example was a food maker that we worked with some years ago. They had to the point of working with us, simply communicated facts about their products. Come and buy from us here. We are open at this time. Our products are made with these ingredients. All of the claims we substantiated, plausible and logical, but they failed to engage emotionally. The food maker was struggling in the face of stiff competition from other artisan businesses in the sector. So we encouraged them to engage their target Personas with things like "try the bread we love"

This was a simple yet very powerful method of showing authenticity and commitment. Facebook has long since moved the word "like" to the new ground zero, the neutral starting point. We knew we had to take our client further and push them beyond their comfort zone of product features and benefits. When they began really committing personally to their communications they realised that their Personas understood and were intrigued about just how good the bread could be. They bought, in significant numbers and volumes. A simple yet logical change in emotional engagement made the necessary difference.

We have tried a similar approach with a number of law firms. The legal sector is one that has transformed over the last few decades. Once the domain of sterile, safe and low impact communications in language that only a trained lawyer would understand, there are now warm, friendly, engaging and customer-centric firms and these are the ones that are leaving the more traditional firms in their wake.

People engage with people. The clue is in the name; social media. The word social gives you all you need to know. People and your Persona specifically, will engage much more.

The key to successful digital advertising, particularly in relation to digital newspapers and magazines, is its ability to bring sound and movement to a traditionally one-dimensional medium.

Web banners

A web banner or banner ad is a form of online advert delivered by an ad server usually at the top of a site page. It consists of an advert embedded into a web page, which when clicked will take the user through to the advertiser's website, known as a 'click through'. The results for advertisement campaigns may be monitored in real-time and may be targeted to the viewer's interests, through online behavioural targeting.

Interstitials

An interstitial advert is one which appears after a user has clicked onto a hyperlink but before the user reaches their intended destination. Such interstitial adverts usually have a mechanism for the user to skip the advert, but these are often obscure and hard to locate.

Superstitial

A superstitial is an interactive, non-banner advert that features animation, sound and graphics. It is usually played when the user takes a break in browsing and plays only when fully loaded. This ensures that every user gets a consistent and complete brand message and that each advertiser pays only for guaranteed impressions.

Pop-ups

Pop-up ads or pop-ups are another form of online advertising, often appearing in a new browser window and usually generated by JavaScript. A variation on the pop-up window is the pop-under advertisement, which opens a new browser window hidden under the active window. This makes it more difficult to determine which website opened them. Most browsers include features to enable users to block pop-ups and/or filter adverts and these are most often set to block by default. With the rapid rise in mobile internet access it is likely that the pop-up advert's days are numbered.

Mobile Advertising display formats extend more traditional forms of digital advertising. There are several types of mobile display advertising that the mobile marketer needs to be aware of and each of which has particular specific strengths.

The mobile marketer needs to be aware of when and where to deploy these effectively. As users feel a very personal affinity to their mobile phones there is considerable opportunity to annoy prospects with inappropriate or ill-timed communications and hence the importance of integrating mobile advertising within a carefully thought through customer journey, engaging at a time convenient to the customer.

Mobile banners
These are horizontal online adverts usually found either across the top or bottom of a mobile device screen in a fixed placement. These adverts are particularly suited to raising awareness within the mobile environment, but in order to do this effectively it is crucial to undertake customer research and analysis beforehand to ensure your ads are being placed on sites and Apps which are relevant to your key customer segments. Banner ads can also be used with a 'call to action' to either gain leads or sales transactions. However, in order for this approach to work effectively, not only do the ads need to be positioned in relevant sites, but they need to be very concise, with impactful creative and a clear benefit for the prospect.

These work most effectively if the promotion is time-restricted to encourage an immediate response.

Mobile Interstitials
This is a web page not requested by a user, containing an advertisement that often opens in a new browser window when the user has clicked on a link within the current page. They can also appear within MMS messages sent to the user. These type of ads need to be used very carefully as there is a high potential of irritating the end user, since they do not ask to see these ads, and it can slow down the task they are trying to achieve, with speed of

achieving tasks being particularly important to users when using the mobile internet out of the home.

Mobile marketers must therefore always check when considering these types of ads that the content that will be displayed offers value to the user: be that relevant information, or entertainment since these ads can be easily dismissed, with the knock-on effect of damaging the advertiser's reputation for responsible customer-focused communications.

In-App adverts

These adverts can be extremely effective as long as the advertiser has taken the time to understand the customer profiles of those using the App, and is offering valued content relevant to their needs. As long as this vital planning step has been undertaken, in-App ads offer advertisers an audience who are already engaged with using the App

If the advertiser is offering a similar or related service, there is a high chance this will appeal to the current App user-base. App customers however are particularly time/task focused as often the purpose of Apps is to achieve certain tasks quicker and more easily than using their related websites, so advertisers need be sure that their offering demonstrates clear value.

For example a restaurant review service could advertise on a location-services App when users search for 'restaurants'. Customers may pay money for ad-free versions of Apps – which underlines the importance of creating engaging ads that clearly demonstrate real customer value.

Mobile video adverts

Using wifi, 3G and 4G technology, it is possible to transmit video adverts, which are growing rapidly in popularity on the 'fixed' internet due to their greater impact and engagement with their target customers.

It is important to understand where mobile communications fit into the overall communication mix and what their advantages are over more traditional forms of advertising and when they can be integrated effectively with other forms of advertising. The customer perspective is always the barometer in the decision.

The main advantages of mobile advertising is the effectiveness in building awareness, with mobile banner ads, a good way to build awareness of related services that may be of interest to users.

For example individual restaurants advertising on a restaurant booking App or mobile website. This should be looked at in the light of the overall communications mix, so should be reinforced via other relevant communication media, both online and offline such as print adverts in local
newspapers and online pay per click adverts.

Mobile adverts can also be used to generate a 'call to action' and hence generate revenue. Using the restaurant example above, a mobile ad could feature a time-limited offer for a restaurant near to the user's location thereby generating a highly relevant and timely offer that may well result in a transaction.

Mobile has the advantage that it can be used to start a conversation and continue engagement through short, relevant micro messages, for example micro-blogs like Twitter or on a brand's Facebook site, asking for a response. In order to generate meaningful response rates, the brand needs to have a pre-existing relationship with the user, whereby the user has expressed an interest in the brand and is open to receiving more communications.

Market feedback and service improvements can be researched by running for example a short Twitter Poll where high responses can be generated from feedback requests that appear very quick and easy to complete.

Lead generation can of course be achieved by mobile communications by attracting prospects' interest to register their interest in a brand, so that they can be followed up later with relevant information. An example would be a car brand advertising on a route-planning website, with the 'call to action' of the ad asking for prospects to register their email address, so that the brand can send more information/ personalised offers.

This could be integrated with more traditional PPC banner adverts, as well as offline adverts such as in magazines.

Competitions and rewards are another valuable engagement tool. Again, the immediacy of the mobile medium makes them more powerful. For example rewards/ loyalty points that can be redeemed in store direct from the mobile device. Competitions can work well in combination with offline media: for example printed scratch-cards which reveal barcodes on winning cards that can be scanned for instant wins which can be redeemed against either online or offline purchases.

One Degree Strategic Digital Marketing Planning Theory

An unnerving thought is that just 1 degree of change in direction can take you to a very different place, in time.

The longer you are mis-pointed or on the wrong non-adjusted course, the further away you are from your desired end destination.

A strategy is like having a compass and a map. You set your destination point using the compass. If you do this in bright daylight with the compass in full view then you are likely to be highly accurate and when you follow the map you reach your destination. This is like strategic planning armed with intelligence, research and a clear understanding of customer needs.

Try plotting a route with your compass and map at night, in poor visibility, and you may make a small margin of error in the magnetic reading of your compass bearing. Over a long distance or time, just one degree variation, will take you to a very different place. This is like running a business or team without a clearly defined destination point, to arrive at a specific time and by taking a particular direction. You will end up somewhere, anywhere, with little or no idea about how you got there.

You may strike lucky without a clearly plotted strategy, but you are much more likely to arrive where you want to be by very accurately plotting a course and then following your strategic compass to your desired destination.

Remember those little 1 degree margins and how you may not notice their effect today, but in time you'll certainly arrive somewhere else.

Consumer Generated Content (sometimes called User Generated Content) CGC is the term used to describe content such as video, blogs, discussion forum posts, digital images, audio files, and other forms of media, created by consumers or end-users of an online system or service.

The vital element is that this information and content is publicly available to other consumers and for the brand to use itself, and repurpose.

Great examples of CGC include where a question is posed by a brand owner in a public online forum and the consumer community begin to add and build a story around the subject, such that the story grows a life of itself.

One of the internet's most significant CGC sites for images is flickr.com which has billions of images and over 2 million communities.

The challenge for the digital marketer seeking to take advantage of the opportunity of CGC, is to devise subjects and innovative ideas that can both stimulate sustainable user generated content at the same time as positioning their brand appropriately within or on the periphery of the discussions.

The marketer might for example, understanding the emotional needs of a target customer persona, create and offer a forum in which that persona community can engage, share and learn from others just like them. The marketer positioning themselves, in this example, as the caring facilitator. In turn this develops trust.

As a key part of a customer's journey, CGC helps them to see the brand as an integral and valuable part of a community that is relevant to them, and not just the vendor of products and services.

In highly commoditised and busy market sectors, cutting through the noise made by marketers clamouring for limited attention of the target customers, can be a thankless task.

CGC is a strategic approach that allows the marketer to position themselves as objective, relevant, current and valuable, in the eyes of the most engaged and potentially profitable customers.

Consider, as an example, an international sales agency in the highly competitive electronics industry. They have the same products to offer as the next sales agent, they have the same level of network and connections and their digital presences is quite generic and akin to their competitors. No amount of advertising or social networking will likely cut through the noise and differentiate them enough to bring them to the awareness of their target prospects and customers.

An agency like this could use CGC to create stories, discussions and innovation. They create an Experts Hub in a distinct area of their website and invite a technical guru from each of the product manufacturers they represent, to be part of a professional portal. This portal allows the technical gurus to pose questions and build discussions and build CGC, without impacting on the resources of the sales agency itself. With an objective position as the facilitator of the Experts Hub, the agency can (if agreed in advance with the invited gurus), publish many of the discussions as white papers, record audio and video interviews and panel discussions and repurpose the content in social media, enticing target prospects and customers into the portal.

As an example of a very low resource method of creating engaging, objective and highly useful content, CGC has a great part to play in the digital marketer's strategic planning as they attempt to scale their reach, cost effectively and in line with their brand evolution.

The biggest challenge is to find what will resonate best with the target audience and those supporters, or in this case, technical experts, who will support and fuel the CGC.

Checklist : Paid, owned and earned media

Integration is key. How will you integrate your online tools with your offline/real world activities?

What balance are you planning between paid, owned and earner media and how do you intend to achieve it?

With the budget you have available for paid marketing, will you achieve your objectives or is there a better way? If so, what is it?

What is your strategy for earned media and how can you

utilise your advocates and influencers to help you achieve it?

What events, launches and news-related content will you publish in the next month to begin your integrated campaigns?

What will you include in your annual campaign plan for the coming year?

9.2 DELIVER : CAMPAIGNS : EMAIL MARKETING

How Noisy is Noisy? Unsubscribe

It has taken nearly two months to rid my inbox of unwanted subscriptions to email databases that I have amassed over recent years.

As we all know, we will be receiving emails from companies that we haven't even heard of as well as from those who have shared our details with third parties. We probably agreed to receive many of these without really noticing and of course when we become a customer of a company they can legally send us emails until we opt out. So over time the noise becomes noisier until you reach your inbox tipping point.

As a consumer, or business customer, we have choices of whether or not to be kept in the loop when a particular company releases some information, news or product and service updates. As a marketer in an ideal world we would like for all our prospects and customers to desire to be on our database so we can send such communications at appropriate intervals.

Herein lies the problem. Good marketers who know their customers and how frequently it is appropriate to contact them are being punished by those who simply send out the 'regular newsletter' on their terms and at their convenience. The bad name that email has received from the customers' perspective over the last decade has been created mostly by those who have considered their own wishes before those of the people they are trying to communicate with. The monologue, promotional style of marketing is so yesterday, and a significant number of 'unsubscribe' results in your email analytics will show you that you are falling into such a trap.

Remember your customers' email inboxes are full and noisy.... very noisy. To ensure that your emails cut through the noise don't just think about catchy titles and lovely images, think about:
  - the time of day when your customers are most receptive, based on their work/life habits
  - the day of the week when they are most likely to have an opportunity to read, absorb, reflect and respond to your messages
  - the frequency by which you send your newsletters. The clue is

the word 'news'. Only send when you have something meaningful to say. Avoid the weekly or monthly schedule
- create a clear call to action for responding to the messages and choreograph the customers' journeys
- always provide an 'unsubscribe' option at the end of every communication you send. It not only gives the recipient choices but it is a legal requirement too.

Beyond the 'awareness creation' stage of the typical digital (and traditional/offline) advertising models we need to integrate our planning and tactics with direct marketing to known customers.

A key tool in this stage of the process is email marketing. With over 500 billion emails being traded across the planet very day (statistics from http://www.radicati.com) we see the extent to which emails dominate our lives.

Email marketing is vital for B2C, B2B and Not for Profit (NFP) organisations of all sizes.

Consider these two examples to see how broad email marketing can be:
i) A large consumer goods company sends special offers to millions of potential
customers, tracks the responses and sends context-sensitive follow up messages with
sophisticated tracking and data collection
ii) A small professional consultancy sends personal emails to senior executives as a
prelude to calling them and seeking a meeting

In fact, it is difficult to think of an organisation which might not use emails in some form or
another as a way of engaging with stakeholders. According to a survey carried out by B2B Marketing, the following statistics applied to UK B2B marketers:

i) Three-quarters had increased their volume of email campaigns and messages in the previous 12 months
ii) Email was regarded as 'important' or 'critical' as a marketing channel by 93% of respondents
iii) The most common objective for email marketing was 'driving

web traffic' (75% of respondents); 'Maintaining customer relationships' was mentioned by 73%; the third most popular objective was 'brand building'

(http://twitter.com/marketingb2b)

Email marketing can be seen as a facet of customer relationship management (CRM) because it is far lower cost than postal equivalent, as a direct response tool it encourages immediate action, campaigns can be put together more quickly, segmentation (especially by response), personalisation, tracking and testing are far easier and more accurate than traditional direct marketing.

In common with postal direct mail, the marketer can expect some resistance to contacting people by e-mail. Not everyone likes to receive mail from organisations, especially if they do not regard themselves as having a need or strong relationship with that organisation. One person's carefully crafted, well targeted e-mail campaign is another's 'junk mail' or 'spam'.

The marketers' biggest challenges then are to ensure the emails are opened, read and acted upon appropriately.

Maximising your chances include:
- Have an enticing subject line
- Consider appropriate length and frequency
- Make it easy to read / include a table of contents, with brief descriptions of what is included and links to more information (usually on your web site)
- Make it personal and casual

An email 'client ' is a piece of software used to manage email campaigns. Anyone contemplating any sort of volume email campaign will need to automate, monitor and measure the campaign in some way, and email clients provide for these features and much more.

Effective starting points for exploring email integration into marketing campaigns include Mailchimp and Hubspot, the latter offering high levels of profiling and measurement along the entire customer journey with direct linking of analytics with the website the email links to.

Whereas websites tend to be a 'pull' technology, where users pull the information off the site when they need it, email tends to be a 'push' technology where content is actively sent to users.

This has both significant advantages and disadvantages for email:
• the ability of marketers to control what information is delivered and when it is delivered is enhanced;
• the delivery of content is at a very low cost;
• modern email clients can offer rich graphical content – virtually to the same level of control as a web page; and
• tracking codes can be inserted to identify when an email is opened and what links are used; but
• the low cost can tempt senders to send more and more frequent emails and users can (and often do) object to being 'bombarded' with emails and overuse of email can result in senders being listed as spammers.

The majority of email marketing has until recently been used to promote websites (on-line to on-line marketing). However there have been significant advances using the email facility on smartphones to send discount codes or vouchers to users' mobiles which can then be used in
retail outlets.

There are a number of key measures used to analyse email effectiveness:
• Open rate – the percentage of subscribers who open an email
• Click rate – what percentage click on a link within the email
• Unsubscribe rate – how many users unsubscribe from a mailing list

I am not saying to avoid purchasing a high quality email database if you are seeking sales leads, but there is a school of thought, of which I am a big supporter, that says a more balanced, content-driven approach should yield better results when growing your business online.

Checklist : Email Marketing

What is your email strategy and how will this appear as tactical marketing activity, integrated with everything else?

Where will you use email in your customer journey? To create initial awareness, or to ongoing communicate with existing customers?

How will you ensure your emails are balanced with the Rule of Thirds and will be perceived as current, relevant and informed?

What specific 'call to action' will you include in your email?

How often will you send your emails? What's the frequency and timing of arrival in the recipients' inbox?

What measurement targets will you set for your email?

10.1 IMPROVE : LISTENING : GOOGLE ANALYTICS

At this point, attention is sure to turn to how best to evaluate the effectiveness of your website and how to improve its design and navigation to maximise transactions, engagement and visitor experience.

Web Analytics is an industry in itself and has set a broad range of conventions and vocabulary such as linking, keywords, stickiness, FAQs, Search Engine Optimisation (SEO), pay-per-click (PPC).

The Digital Analytics Association (DAA) has created standards for measures and the definition of web analytics as "the measurement, collection, analysis and reporting of internet data for the purposes of understanding and optimizing web usage."

The early web counter can still be found on some websites and is still a badge of honour for
You Tube who show the number of hits of the most popular videos and on Twitter for the number of Followers. However on professional business websites the counter has become uncommon, as more complex information can now be derived from visitor activity through the likes of Google Analytics.

Behind every web site there is a computer server which was normally located in the IT department at the company's offices, but now with the rapid growth of Wordpress (the world's most prolific website hosting platform) is more likely to be in the cloud.

The server 'serves' any requested information to the website visitor through their chosen browser (software on their device).

For marketers measuring activity on their website it is all about your customers' journey and how the server reports this activity to Google Analytics software which 'listens' to every pocket of activity throughout your site.

The trick is to measure the effectiveness of each and every communication point in terms of how much trust and commitment you score in the eyes of your customer. Trust and commitment equates to real engagement and that has some value points.

At key moments in the customer journey (especially where the customer makes a decision, acts upon a call to action, or enters into a transaction) the value points accumulate. Plot the value of each of those key moments in terms of how much it contributes to the overall journey and multiply up by a weighting of your top priority customers or customer segments.

The result will be a customer journey that shows where the most important points are for each top priority customer and how you are actually performing in their eyes. That is real marketing measurement and you will never worry about vanity metrics again. Google calls this the Visitor Flow and it is becoming ever prominent in the dashboards that are presented to the marketer after their Google Analytics login.

For many years we have heard the term 'stickiness' used in relation to web sites. If a web site is sticky then we attract a visitor and keep them looking at our site, hopefully they will take some action such as requesting further information or placing an order. Sticky is therefore to be encouraged.

Web analytics also has a word to describe the opposite of stickiness and that is the word
'bounce'. Bounce occurs when a visitor arrives at a web page then leaves the site effectively with a single page visit.

For example, a bounce rate of 67% means that 67% of visitors took one look at the page and decided it was not for them. Only a third of visitors decided to look further into the site. This can be interpreted in many ways. One interpretation is that "I have been promoting my website to the wrong people, I may have paid for the wrong 'keywords' or I may have given misleading descriptions in my pages or in the hidden messages I write for search engines". Another interpretation is "that my 'entry pages' are badly designed; I need to modify them to create something far more interesting".

Commentators may say that a bounce rate above 50% on a specific page is concerning. However, some specific pages, such as blogs and case studies, especially when used as a landing page within a customer retention campaign, see high bounce rates because the visitor is already very familiar with the content on other pages on the site or is just dipping in for breaking news.

It is therefore important to say that whilst bounce rate is a key performance indicator in website analytics it should be used in conjunction with other measures to give a well-rounded view.

As marketers we are all taught about 'Segmentation, Targeting and Positioning'. We must divide the population into similar groups. Only then can we decide what targets to select.

Once we have a target or several targets, we can then position our product in the mind of the prospect. Web Analysts have taken the aspect of 'segmentation' (although targeting and positioning are not mentioned in those terms). Careful focus, targeting and responsible planning to provide different measures, analytics and ultimately different customer journeys across the various segments allows for good control of bounce rate.

As well as social media signposting, arguably the most important method of driving traffic to a website is an effective search engine position.

This can take many forms from simply good website design using a large number of appropriate long tail key words in the content, to paid position for a fee (pay-per-click or pay per impression) advertising.

Earlier forms of search engines deeply analysed keywords buried inside the coding for the pages, and meta tags or descriptions and titles. Search engines have now developed into sophisticated automated applications that 'read' the content and images of the website and position each site according to the appropriateness of its content relative to others. Such applications include 'robots' and 'spiders' which regularly revisit sites for reassessment. Recently the major search engines have become semantic search tools, listening and learning from the interrelated content throughout a site and how it relates to other sites in its category.

Search Engine Optimisation (SEO) is the process of getting the best ranking for a website. Ideally on the first page of the search results as most visitors only look at the first or possibly second page of search engine results.

Websites, images, video and other online communication media such as PDFs are displayed by search engines through complex algorithmic processes of which SEO is a composite, contributing by trying to improve the volume of traffic to the website by optimising the relevance of the results of the search, and by more accurate targeting to the specific enquiries.

SEO refers to organic searches as opposed to sponsored links. SEO is the 'natural' relevancy of a website for a particular product or information source in relation to others. The latter is paid for advertising.

SEO Warfare

"I was recently speaking to Panda Doc about our online forms for BBP and came across 2 companies that seem to have bought Panda Doc's company name as their own Google Adwords. Their own businesses now show up above PandaDoc's page by using their own trading name." Neil Smith BBPMedia

This interesting example typifies some of the so-called black hat SEO techniques where subtle yet extremely powerful tricks are used to effectively block out the competition. But just how far would you take yours?

For everyone who knows a little about how these things work this kind of technique appears underhand, sly and to be honest, a bit devious? Instead of relying on authentic value of your own offering and trusting that it's strong enough to appeal and attract visitors to your site or social network pages, this could easily be perceived as simply not playing the game fairly?

If the technique is designed to attract the unsuspecting who don't realise the difference between paid and owned media, then the word devious could certainly apply. I don't believe it's fair to say that anything goes, in digital warfare. We should still maintain integrity and honour and if our product and service messages aren't strong enough then we can always take a look in the mirror and make appropriate improvements to them.

By doing this we will ensure the credibility of our brand and its values are maintained.

Like everything in business and marketing, a strategic approach is required when considering appropriate SEO targets to measure. These could include the objective the website wants to attain (landing page visits, sales transactions, referrals or recommendations), taking on board the type of product service or information the website has to offer and what kind of search engines to concentrate on.

Search Engines are increasingly important due to a combination of socio-cultural and technological lifestyle reasons: people are more time precious, in part due to an increasing array of leisure choices available. Our access and reliance on internet interconnectivity is becoming more and more pervasive with wifi-connected cities and prevalence of high speed mobile internet.

Each search engine has its own set of algorithms which it does not disclose, although most will give pointers to what approaches site owners can take to optimise their rankings in organic/natural search.

Nobody knows the exact combination of factors that give the ideal search ranking.

It had generally been considered that websites appear higher in search rankings when metatags (information inserted into the 'head' area of your web pages) containing keywords are present. Metadata is useful as this will be seen by the searcher when the page results are presented, hence a sensible choice of terms, especially page titles is important. It's not however, a determinant in how Google ranks.

Inbound links had been the most important single factor rated by Google, but in more recent times, the importance of links has been downgraded heavily in favour of original, fresh, long-tail content and especially that with a geographic (town, city, country) reference.

Getting Started with Google Analytics

Quick introductions to Google Analytics often begin with a confusing trawl through the myriad of website data, trends and graphs. This can cause chaos for even the most experience marketing team because it so easy to become quickly bogged down by the volume of website data.

A more logical and succinct approach is to take three steps:

Step 1 - Have a quick look at the basic features of the Google Analytics dashboard and administration screens to get a flavour of the types of information available

Step 2 - Brainstorm a prioritised list of the answers you need to be able to make sound business and marketing decisions

Step 3 - Using the most important answers in your list, go back into Google Analytics and ask the questions of it that are most likely to give you the answers you need
Think : What intelligence will help me to do something differently if I knew the answer? If I have a perfect navigation through my website for my customer, what journey would that be? Have I avoided the obvious vanity metrics like Number of Visitors to My Website!? Because these mean nothing

Step 1 is simple. You login and have a general look around at the dashboards and click through the menu in the left hand column which acts as your main navigation through the service. Try clicking on Admin towards the top right hand corner of the page and see your account settings, views and importantly the various tools and widgets you'll use later.

Step 2 is tricky. Take post-its, pens and some time to write out all the various questions you'd like answers for from your website. If your website could talk what would you ask it. Think of things that really matter to you and your business decisions. Think up everything you can for each of the stages of the customer journey. We should be able to work out the questions once you know the answers you need.

Step 3 is hard. Armed with the answers you need it's time to work out what questions to ask of Google Analytics to turn the information inside into useful intelligence to aid your decision making. Try thinking of the following mantra: Sources (your audience or visitors) Behaviours (and customer journey) Conversion (to see if they did what you expected or wanted them to do) and create your dashboard and shortcuts to quickly return to the latest data and trends next time.

Sources- Google calls this Audience and Acquisition and it

focuses on where your visitors came from, what search phrases they used, their location, if they came via a social network and whether they are on a mobile or computer.

Behaviours - Google includes pages per visit, time spent in the site, drop out rates and visitor flow, the pages they visited in step by step. For this you can use in-page analytics to see the % of click throughs on each link on every page. Follow the route your customers are taking to better understand their experience.

Conversion - Set goals in your Admin area that reflect what you need as a business and they will appear in your website reports and dashboard. You will easily see the % completion of each goal.

Two clever things about Google Analytics is that you can combine any of the above into a custom report so you can construct highly targeted performance analysis that reflect the detailed visitor profiles you wish to attract. This can, where data exists, include the different behaviours of visitors based on their age, location and gender. Simply click on the 'Add to Dashboard' or 'Shortcut' to favourite any custom report you create.

If you do not have the time to keep logging into Google Analytics you can easily create Custom Alerts in your Admin screen that will email you when your specified goals are reached. And working as a team? Each team member can create their own Private Dashboard using the '+ New Dashboard' link at the top of the left navigation panel.

Total customisation and even real-time visitor analysis if you have a very busy website. Google Analytics remains the best in class website analysis tool.

Checklist : Google Analytics

How do you intend to avoid vanity metrics when assessing your website performance?

Do you need to watch real-time performance of your website or will retrospective measurement be appropriate?

What measures will you regularly monitor for understanding your audience and the visitors to your website?

Which channels will you monitor in the acquisition reports to see where the visitors to your website are coming from?

Is the balance of new versus returning visitors appropriate to your marketing strategy?

What behaviours do you need to monitor as your visitors journey through your website?

Can you replicate your desired customer journey with the actual visitor behaviour through your website?

Have you set conversion targets to determine the outcomes of your visitors behaviours?

10.2 IMPROVE : LISTENING : SOCIAL MEDIA INSIGHTS

ICE Model for Testing Social Media Effectiveness

Intelligence, Communication, Evaluation; the three key steps in measuring the effectiveness of your social networking.

Through this winter we will see more and more organisations both large and small realising that they cannot just simply 'do' social networking. They will realise that they need to ensure they are doing the right social networking, testing all the time what works and what doesn't and then changing behaviour patterns, frequency, networks, tone and style to see better and better outcomes.

Using the acronym ICE we have three simple steps that can help plan, act and improve everything we do and here's how you can get started:

Intelligence
This is the part most people pass by. Getting the right intelligence at the outset is key to setting out in the right direction with content, images and videos all of which can engage and influence your target audience.

As a simple rule of thumb you need to know what will hook your audience from both a practical and an emotional level. Irrespective of what you want or need to say, promote or share you need to know what the audience want to hear.

A good example are the list of Interests of your social networks. These are the things that those in your networks have put as interests in their profiles, are discussing with their friends or colleagues or even clicking on in advertisements. Interests ensure that you don't always talk about what YOU want to talk about but engage with others on their terms. Show a little interest in the other person and the favour will be returned.

Helpful online tools for finding out the Interests of those in your networks include Social Report and Sprout Social It is much easier to let these tools do the hard work than you look at each and every connection to try to work out what to say.

If you have some geographic element in your communication head to Map My Followers to see where in the country or world your followers are situated and prioritise and tune your messages accordingly.

Combining this intelligence with the professions of your followers using Demographics Pro can help you to add on top of the emotional hooks some practical, job or industry specific content and messages.

There are of course many more tools and approaches and examples of the types of intelligence you need to collect. Your own selection will be based on your clear understanding of the audience profiles, or as we call them personas, because they are real people, not companies or brands. Knowing exactly who they are will help you to work out what you need to find out about them.

Communication
Using the intelligence we move into the Communication stage. This is when we begin to test out what we know in our social networks. We produce content, images and videos that really do talk to our target audiences about things they are interested in. It's not about what WE want to say, it's about what THEY want to hear.

Keeping a close watch on the outcomes from everything you post, share or say is key to this phase. Every time you do something in social media you need to know why you are doing it. What is your desired outcome from what you just did? If it's not adding some value to the longer term goals then why did you do it? Don't get swept along by hype, the next big thing or the latest technology. Stay true to your strategy and keep focused.

If you see a pattern develop either positively or negatively for specific types of content you share then you need to act on that and do more of it if it's good or stop doing it if it's not working.

Some of the most popular tools for keeping a close watch on these trends (not responses or lack of responses to individual posts or actions, you need to see patterns before you change anything) include Hootsuite and here are a selection of others.

Remember it's also about the Rule of Thirds at this stage. It's not about you, it's about them. But you do get a chance to sell through social media if you have added value first.

Evaluation

If Intelligence is an often overlooked stage, then Evaluation is the grand daddy of opportunity that most regularly goes missing. Evaluation is all about the simple concept of learning from what happened so you can improve what you'll do next time. It sounds obvious but we see countless examples of people and organisations who continuously battle on doing the same old errors and knowing something is wrong but not quite what it is.

There are lots of simple digital dashboards which joined together can give you that all important means of continuous improvement. At a basic level there are Facebook Insights and Linkedin Insights.

Of course just fine tuning your content is all very well but what about the actual outcomes? The new business leads and additional visitors to your website? There is still nothing better than Google Analytics for watching not only who comes into your website and through which social network but vitally, what did they do after they landed. Which pages did they go to next and what happened then? With a pre-planned customer journey in your strategy you can help these social network contacts through the myriad of messages and noise in your marketing so they arrive right at the end point. It is there that they'll give you that return on your investment of time and energy.

The ICE acronym is a fast and simple checklist to ensure that you don't just 'do' social networking but that you are in the right place at the right time, saying the right things to the right people for the right reasons and getting the right outcomes in line with your goals.

As we consider measuring the length of our customers' journey, social media monitoring can provide us with a valuable insight into the views and opinions of our prospects and customers.

Google Analytics will only show us what is happening within the boundaries of our website. Beyond this we need to look deeply into our social media insights.

These can offer rapid feedback on advertising and promotional campaigns, a quick easy way to provide customer support and assistance, and a means to track commentary on the organisation and to act upon it if necessary.

Each activity requires different skills and tools to provide suitable results. Marketing and feedback monitoring requires regular scheduled reporting of responses (both comments and click throughs).

Customer support requires more real-time information and a search facility to ensure timely responses.

The majority of social media tracking products and in-built insights, are web or cloud based applications with both a free and subscribed element. For each organisation it is likely that a combination of live activity and off-line reporting functions will be required because the customers journey is most likely to have both online and offline elements.

There are five distinct advantages to social network marketing that make it a vital and highly measurable tool to include in a marketing campaign:

1. Better targeting – social network marketing can draw a highly targeted segment of customers to visit a business or website, increasing visibility of content on both a local and global level.

2. High return on investment – social network marketing is one of the cheapest ways of marketing currently available providing a potentially high return on investment. Low budget investment means lower risk to even the smallest business. However, returns on investment need to take into account wider resource commitment of people's time in order to fully understand the true return on marketing investment.

3. Does not require technical skills – most social networking sites are visually oriented and user-focused, which means anyone can use the tools. Time spent monitoring and adapting needs to be borne in mind as each network adopts its own methods it becomes a constant learning curve.

4. Increases cut-through – because most internet users are bombarded with adverts every day, people are starting to become

less receptive to them. Social network marketing provides a personalised view point to attract potential customers to the things that interest them. Social networking sites, including Facebook, have targeted text advertising with fees aimed at small businesses. LinkedIn's fees can be as low as a few dollars for 1,000 impressions and allow advertisers to set small budgets, which in turn allow for flexibility, A/B testing and changes at short notice to ensure advert optimisation. Advertisers can also choose different criteria to target, including geography, industry, seniority and company size.

Social network marketing is not a financial burden but can be resource heavy, with time being a crucial aspect to a successful campaign.

5. Increased visibility – Social network marketing can help to spread information. and can therefore be used by marketers to help build stronger and deeper relationships, if the marketer identifies which platforms work best for them and concentrate their efforts. It constantly comes back to segmentation and targeting of the most profitable persona. For the long term, the value for marketing on social networking sites may be simply the ability to reach niche groups via advertising on the site and spread information.

Each social network has their own Insights showing a wealth of statistics and performance metrics for the marketers' connections/ followers behaviour. However a wider, integrated digital dashboard may show the inter-relation between activities and a more cohesive 'journey long' set of data from which information can be turned into decision-supporting intelligence.

Checklist : Social media insights

Have you set targets and smart goals for each social network?

What do you need to know about how and when your connections are engaging with your content and which content works best?

Which content has stimulated and attracted new connections and followers and why?

How responsive are you to incoming messages, comments and enquiries?

Avoiding vanity metrics, are your connections and followers appropriate to helping you achieve your higher level marketing goals?

What time of the day and day of the week is the most effective to publish content in each social network?

Have your calls to action achieved their goals and what can you do to improve the conversion rate of each?

What are you learning from your competitors' activities that you can avoid or integrate into your future social networking?

Have you identified the most important measures to include in your digital dashboard?

10.3 : IMPROVE : LISTENING : SOCIAL LISTENING

Google Analytics for your digital hub, website, is great and social media insights are excellent measures of how you are performing within the community of your followers and connections.

However, what is going on beyond your connections in the wider world of digital and communications? The only way of knowing this is to practice ongoing social listening and keep abreast of what is being discussed about you, your brand and your campaigns.

Social Mention .com is a great resource to monitor positive and negative mentions of what you choose to search on and acts in real time as well as historically.

This means you have the opportunity for responding to both positive and negative conversations and posts that are beyond your current connections and followers, whenever you need to.

This form of social listening ensures you can always react quickly and proactively to opportunities and minimise the impact of negative comment in proactive crisis management.

Contingency Planning in Digital Marketing

I once met a military man who had an interesting perspective on life and business. He always had a way out, an exit, a second option. In marketing we call this a contingency plan. In his world he called it survival.

We met in a restaurant to talk about business as he had moved into commercial acquisitions since leaving his special forces life behind but I could see from the first hand shake that he was different.

He needed to sit with his back to the room so that he could survey everything with one glance, at any moment he wanted. He clearly knew where the door was and the quickest route to get there.

This was a man so finely honed in the art of survival it had become an instinct.

At no point in the meeting was he truly at ease. He was on a mission, with a clear objective and only fleetingly did he allow himself the luxury of deviation from his course.

I felt this was a shame because it didn't allow him a chance to express, to take unplanned risks or explore creative solutions. To him the mission was set, and he could execute it, safe in the knowledge that if the first planned option was about to fail he could instantly revert to Plan B or make a hasty exit and be gone.

As we talked, he shared how he was using his past training to great effect in business, buying, building then selling commercial assets and each time with 1. a defined and clear exit strategy, and 2. a contingency plan. The idea of exploring and just seeing how things turn out was as alien to him, as to me, his continuous surveying of the room for an enemy.

We were very much like chalk and cheese, polar opposites and yet in the middle we met with a mutual respect that we were comfortable in our own ways of approaching a commercial relationship. The one element we shared in common was our appreciation of contingency plans. The Plan B.

Rather than a sign of low confidence in Plan A, a contingency plan accepts the inevitability of the known unknown and vitally, the unknown unknown, which can appear at any point and in any guise. To be able to make choices on alternative options wherever you are in life and business based on a pre-planned set of considered second choice routes, just makes sense.

I may not be looking to win battles like my military friend but having contingencies allows me to sleep at night without the need to keep one eye open and that works for me.

Checklist : Social listening

Do you have continuous visibility of all mentions of your brand, products and services, across the internet?

What is your level of responsiveness to positive and negative mentions, comments, and shares of your content, outside of your immediate network?

What keywords and phrases have you identified that are most associated with your content and that you can use in future articles, posts and updates?

How are you continually monitoring the impact and reach of your campaigns, product news and blogs?

What competitors' activities are you monitoring and learning from in their performance across the internet?

11.1 IMPROVE : SHARE : INFORMATION INTO INTELLIGENCE

It is quite difficult now to keep up with the myriad of changes that are taking place in digital marketing and social media. Every day there are news announcements of what Facebook and the others are up to, what is happening on YouTube and Twitter and how Instagram and Pinterest are constantly punching above their weight for media attention.

The beauty of realising that no matter how hard you try you will never be at the cutting edge of this wave of new marketing opportunity, is that you relax and begin to focus on the things that really matter: the trends, the networks and the people who will actually make a difference to your organisation and the profits it so desperately needs in these difficult times.

What we need is a dashboard that allows us to focus on what really counts and the things that will both make a difference to your customers' journey and lifetime value at the same time as creating profitable new business and value for your organisation. This is the essence and goal of marketing.

We begin by setting the baseline with an initial audit of both the organisation and its competitors to help establish the current situation that forms the platform for future improvement and enhancement.

Ensuring you have a presence in a wide range of appropriate social networks, in discussion groups and forums as well as through your newsletters and website are of course key elements in your marketing mix. The idea of future proofing yourself today by taking ownership and continually reinforcing key long tail phrases in everything you talk about is a great way of becoming relevant to your target audiences, customers and prospects.

So now it's time to check how you are doing and it starts quite simply. Create your current Word Cloud using a service such as www.tagxedo.com, a simple content-focused marketing cloud that will show you by the relative sizes of words and phrases, exactly what it is you are currently publishing through social media, your website and more. If you find some surprises you can then fine-tune your emphasis to ensure what you are saying is aligned to your strategy.

The purpose of measurement for digital campaigns is the same as the purpose of measuring more traditional forms of marketing. It is to:

1. Measure marketing productivity
2. Examine return on marketing investment (ROMI)
3. Evaluate customer satisfaction and involvement
4. Measure market share and forecast demand

The majority of problems in measuring offline marketing success stem from the lack of immediacy between the marketing activity and the action, and also from the inability to directly and cost effectively collect, collate and interpret any link between the activity and the action. In many cases the key problem is the cost of collecting suitable data.

Additionally the vast majority of organisations will be running more than one marketing activity at a time and so any increase in enquiry, footfall, or sales could be attributed to any or all of these activities.

Ideally, in order to separate the effects of each marketing activity a business would have only one activity at a time, then collect the results and assess the effectiveness. In the offline world this is clearly impossible but on the internet it might be achievable, as with effective tracking and analysis it can separate the effects of different simultaneous campaigns.

Let's begin with the curse of poor digital marketing metrics, the vanity metric.

The easiest things to measure are often irrelevant. We call these 'vanity metrics': visitors to your website, the number of Twitter followers, impressions on a Facebook posting, the circulation figures for a magazine in which you have an article... the list goes on.

Why are these things pointless? Because less might be more. If the numbers are large they are likely to include people who have no real interest in you, your products and services. The recent publicity over

Subscription services where anyone can buy Twitter followers points to the hollowness of some metrics.

Awareness is pointless if it does not result in a positive sentiment, action or a 'sale'. A Marketing Multiplier gets you thinking about the real deal, the places where you can make a difference to your highest priority customers, the ones who will help you deliver proper value and return on investment.

It is all about your customer journey along the Sales Funnel: the step-by-step process along which you are guiding your customer in your communications.

The trick is to measure the effectiveness of each and every communication point in terms of how much trust and commitment you score in the eyes of your customer. Trust and commitment equates to real engagement and that has some value points. At key moments in the customer journey (especially where the customer makes a decision, acts upon a call to action, or enters into a transaction) the value points accumulate. Plot the value of each of those key moments in terms of how much it contributes to the overall journey and multiply up by a weighting of your top priority customers or customer segments. The result will be a customer journey that shows where the most important points are for each top priority customer and how you are actually performing in their eyes.

That is real marketing measurement and you will never worry about vanity metrics again.

So now, in order for the effectiveness of digital marketing to be accurately analysed it is essential that any marketing activity meets the following criteria:

1. The marketing needs to have clearly defined success criteria
2. The call(s) to action need to be clear and unambiguous
3. There need to be effective means to track the customer path through the marketing activity to the desired end result
4. The collection and analysis of this data has to be cost-effective and timely

For the vast majority of on-line marketing the company website is the chosen destination for the customers and this is the most mature field of on-line marketing. Therefore the majority of developments in on-line analysis has been in this area.

But how do you evaluate the effectiveness of your website? How do you improve its design?

The answer lies in web analytics – the industry that has developed to measure and analyse internet data, bringing a new set of tools and jargon. It has a professional body – the Digital Analytics Association (DAA), with conferences, an education programme and standards for measures.

The Official DAA Definition of Web Analytics is: "the measurement, collection, analysis and reporting of internet data for the purposes of understanding and optimizing web usage."

Common measures include click through rate (CTR), the percentage of viewers of an advert/marketing opportunity that make the first 'click' through to the target media. Within Pay Per Click advertising this metric rapidly identifies the initial success of any advert and is used by both the advertiser and publisher to select the best adverts.

We also monitor bounce rate, the percentage of viewers who initially click on an advert then immediately 'bounce' back to the originating website (or any other website). A high bounce rate may indicate a poorly targeted advert or content of low interest.

There is also the conversion rate, the percentage of viewers who subsequently complete the transaction to whatever is defined as a success by the advertiser (this is usually, though not always, a sale).

Cost per click, which is usually associated with paid website adverts such as Google Adwords, boosted posts on Facebook, or Promoted Tweets, can be used to assess the results of other marketing activities provided clicks can be attributed accurately.

Similarly within the email arena, the key measures used to analyse email effectiveness are the open rate, the percentage of subscribers who open an email. There is also the click rate, the percentage who click on a link within the email and unsubscribe rate which shows how many recipients unsubscribe from a mailing list.

Bounce rate, emails that are 'bounced' back undelivered by the recipients' mail servers, is similar to the rate of undelivered and returned mail with a physical mail drop. However once a link within an email has been clicked, any further 'bounces' refer to the act of the recipient returning immediately from the website.

It should be noted that most email marketing relies on tagging links and images with additional codes (or script) that is activated when the email is opened (and so requests images or code) and when links are clicked. Many email clients will automatically refuse to download images with tracking codes and so the open rate and click rate for email marketing are often large underestimates.

When the marketer is some way along their decision making process about the most appropriate digital tools for a campaign they must in parallel consider measurement. Campaign measurement is becoming ever more important in the drive for value, cost effectiveness and in the light of tight marketing budgets.

The marketer should start with a focus on setting objectives within a clear process and as such there are six steps in the Campaign Creation Model.

i) Target Audience – a critical starting point helping you to define exactly who you are talking to. Who is your key audience in the campaign and which other customer segment might benefit from hearing your messages too?

ii) Objectives – you cannot run an effective campaign without establishing your targets at the outset. What are your strategic targets, the ones that will help you to deliver your bigger organisational goals? What key performance indicators are you going to use so you can monitor how the campaign is progressing and check the success at the end?

iii) Messages – what is the lead message or proposition for this campaign? What back-up messages will support the lead message? Are these consistent with other campaigns you have run or are running and consistent with your brand?

iv) Creative – what electronic and printed materials do you need for your campaign? Have you factored the cost of producing and delivering these into your campaign plan? The costs of these need to be included in your objectives because if you over spend the profitability of your campaign will reduce.

v) Channels – how will your target audience experience your campaign? Where will they see, hear and sample it? Think both traditional channels like PR, advertising and direct mail as well as electronic channels such as web, email and social media. Join all your delivery channels together in a nice simple visual so that everyone knows where your campaign is happening and what is expected as an outcome from each element.

vi) Timing – everything at each step needs to be time bound, so set some realistic yet challenging timescales for each element above. Identify your start date and target end date but remember to build in a review stage so you can analyse and learn from the outcomes and results of your campaign.

This process is simplistic and needs to be adapted to fit with the selected tools and approach but is an easy and SMART (specific, measurable, achievable, realistic, time-bound) method of starting things off.

Ongoing evaluation of what does and does not work is essential feedback in the rolling strategy e-marketing planning process. Elements to consider include volume of unique visitors to the site, the number of sales enquiries, volume and value of transactions, advertising click-through rates across various third party advertisements, the impact of offline campaigns and online campaigns and direct email measurements and conversion rates. It is only through a direct 'return on investment' analysis that the true worth of the e-marketing commitment can be assessed.

To achieve this we need to focus on integrating our measurement and our reporting.

Integration is not about matching luggage, it is about ensuring that every individual customer's touchpoint to a brand not only works in isolation, but also builds on a message.

For a new James Bond film many consumers might just see a poster, so it needs to stand alone. Replicating that poster on TV, however would be ineffective and unrewarding, so something extra is required. A great trailer supports the poster you have seen, but also builds on the story. Again, some may only see that trailer, so it is essential that integration is about making each media work on its own, but also ensuring that they build on one another. Each piece of communication should have continuity, but also the same intensity of message.

As we have seen, online works within integrated campaigns to not only raise awareness, but stimulate word of mouth and create stories. It is particularly effective for tactically drip feeding elements to the consumer to build and maintain a buzz ahead of release.

So if integration is about reaching your audience wherever they are online or offline, the challenge for marketers is to identify at the outset, exactly what it is they are managing.

Channels should not be determined by what is available, but what is being used the most by your key audience and both offline and online need to feed off of each other.

Vanity Metrics : The Lazy Digital Marketer's Tool

Vanity metrics are the ideal tool for the lazy marketer. A quick glimpse at the number of followers, a glance at your likes or a cursory nod to the volume of visitors to the home page of your website in a busy working day can feel like an adequate measure of your progress.

But what a lazy approach. By simply looking at the surface of your website, digital marketing and social media analytics, all you will see is the equivalent of the length of the queue coming to a party at your home, arriving at your front door and making it into the hallway. Does this really tell you if your visitors liked what they saw and if they felt there was enough value to stay around a while? Will it show you which rooms they moved into and what they did in there? And if you were inviting them to the party, did they linger enough to enter into a conversation and did they enjoy themselves enough to sample your food and drink. In other words did you gain a real friend?

The analogy of inviting guests to a party at your home is so similar to encouraging people into your social networks or onto your website.

You would never just think of the success of your party as the size of your guest list or how great your invitations were so let's not stop our marketing at the email newsletter or the tweet.

Friends and colleagues wouldn't be talking about your party for months to come by the quality of your front door or hallway, so we shouldn't just measure our website visitor volumes or Facebook likes, or Twitter followers.

Our party would be rated about the level of engagement our guests had with each other, so in digital we can measure conversations; their sentiment and quality.

The food and drink at our party is the equivalent of our products and services. Present those well and people will sample and come back for more.

So in essence we should be measuring the entire length of the customer journey. From the initial awareness, through each stage of engagement to the point where the customer becomes a loyal advocate and invites others to the party themselves.

In your website Google Analytics will call this your Goal Conversions. On Facebook this might be Reach and Engagement. In wider social media, outside of your networks you might need Social Mention to ascertain positive, neutral and negative comments and discussions.

The next time you feel yourself falling asleep at the wheel and becoming the next lazy marketer, ask yourself if you can prove that everyone who came to your party enjoyed themselves. Not everyone will, but at least you'll know who did, who didn't, why and what you can do to improve your party next time.

Remembering that the success of an integrated marketing campaign is reliant on the continuous fuelling of it, long tail, relevant content is key and as such blogs perform exceptionally well on search engines because of their frequency and freshness, which search engines such as Google have as a key criteria for search.

Secondly the content of blogs tends to be written in search engine optimised copy (as opposed to brochure speak) and people increasingly use search engines using everyday language rather than keywords.

The third search criteria used by search engines is popularity, looking for popular websites which search engines ascertain as the websites with the most links to and from them. Business websites, as such, tend not to have as many links to or from their websites as blogs do.

Therefore, in any short burst campaign, a blog or micro blog (Twitter) should be at the heart of the campaign and particularly if the objective is raising awareness in the eyes of the target market recruitment. Measuring not only incoming engagement but also where that engagement then leads allows for continuous improvement and enhancement of both the customer journey and the end transaction at the completion of the marketing process. For this we need conversion funnel analytics.

Conversion or sales, funnels are often used in A/B Testing. If for example, we are testing two campaign approaches, one of the campaigns is centred on low price but the other on quality. We need to create two executions of a web page, one for each campaign, and the web server is told to alternate the viewing: so A goes to the first visitor, B to the second, A to the third and so on. Then a conversion funnel is created for both options and we can see the difference. This is simple but effective experimentation.

By setting clear objectives right the way through the conversion funnel journey the digital marketer is able to test and improve outcomes continuously in a controlled manner and thereby improve return on investment to the organisation.

At the heart of this A/B testing is the need to define and establish very clearly exactly the point of conversion in the customer/sales journey because ultimately everything points to that from the transition of prospect into customer.

All websites have a purpose, and usually it is to persuade the visitor to carry out some action: Read an article; Sign up to a newsletter; Request a brochure; Make contact; Place an order.

When this objective is achieved, we can call it a conversion, the ultimate goal of our marketing, testing, analytics and reporting.

Checklist : Information into intelligence

What is your plan and process for turning the data from website, social media and wider analytics and measurement into useful decision-making intelligence?

Have you accurately aligned what you are saying with your longer term business vision?

Are you regularly A/B testing everything you do digitally to ensure you are continuously improving?

Have you consciously avoided vanity metrics and are you making sound, evidence-based decisions?

What new macro trends can you integrate into your future marketing strategy and tactical plans?

How will you maintain competitive advantage on an ongoing basis?

12.1 IMPROVE : INNOVATE : CUSTOMER RELATIONSHIP MANAGEMENT

Closely associated with the planning of relevant communities, campaigns and marketing activity is the formation of suitable databases for customer relationship management (CRM) purposes.

Databases can take varied and numerous forms and are often very closely aligned to sales records and customers' purchasing behaviours. The more relevant information that can be captured about how, when and why a customer interacts with the organisation, the more the data can inform great decision making.

This decision making is at the very core of good CRM practice. The more accurate and recent the data, the better the intelligence that can be gleaned from it and used to continuously improve the customer experience, internal practices, new products and services and enhanced systems and operations.

Databases and CRM records are often captured and manipulated in Marketing Information Systems (MIS) and shared widely across the organisation and used effectively in management decision making.

Where there are disparate databases, it is the marketer's responsibility to ensure they are integrated wherever possible to provide added value to the organisation. A great starting point in this activity is to focus on the customer journey. This end to end, step by step, map of engagement helps to focus the data capture to a granular level and as such it means that every opportunity for improvement is captured and identified.

At a tactical level there are mostly three levels of digital measurement that can feed the databases and CRM systems:

- Google Analytics for website analysis and assessment
- Social Media Insights to capture the activities, reach and engagement of social networks
- Wider online insights and mentions (www.socialmention.com) for data beyond the digital horizon

To achieve consistency and meet objectives when considering all of the above, having suitable control and measurement systems in place is of vital importance. Management Information Systems (MIS) constantly and consistently fed by market, product, price, customer, supplier and competitor information will help to produce accurate and timely statistics and reports that will help to fine tune campaigns and input intelligence into strategy.

Databases that are automatically updated by content management systems and transactions are preferable to any manual intervention and although probably more costly are able to output significantly more detailed reports and statistical analysis.

What do you put onto your dashboard of things to watch, measure and analyse? Simply the things that matter most. A balance of financial, marketing, innovative and process things that can feed upward to deliver your marketing goals and to your organisational goals beyond.

If you are not watching then you cannot measure and if you do not measure you cannot prove the return on your investment of time, resource and budget and if you cannot do that then competitors will quite rightly steal business and customers and social media engagement from right under your nose.

Clear product branding is therefore critical in the online environment. Product branding is a set of value propositions that communicate to a customer the benefits of a particular product or service. Product branding also communicates the seller's promise to deliver a specific set of features, benefits or services. Because there is no physical or personal presence a product brand is a critical element of the e-mix. The total product (all the elements that make up the range of benefits offered by that product, as perceived by the customer) must be considered in its entirety.

A digital dashboard is a central place where a marketer can see at a glance a range of information that helps them turn data into intelligence to inform their decision making. Good decisions help to grow a business, reduce risk in an organisation and ultimately provide better customer journey and marketing service.

It is very easy to collect data. The skill behind effective dashboards is to measure things that help you to learn and improve and turn that data into decision making tools. To do this it is important to blend and integrate not only the hard numbers but softer, subjective measures that can often give a broader context to why the numbers are as they are.

Trends are important too. To see a piece of data in isolation and reporting a situation in a fixed point in time is unlikely to give a clear indication of the scenario. A dashboard that reports over set periods, again tied into the decision-making schedule, is far more likely to demonstrate fluctuations and trends from which improvements can be made.

The starting point in digital dashboard planning is to understand your over-arching objectives. Strategic and their supporting tactical goals, will help to identify the kinds of data and information that need to feed into the dashboard. This filtering process in itself helps you to ensure you are only including information that will actually help you. With the proliferation of available data from the likes of the popular Google Analytics, you can literally become swamped by information. In good digital dashboard creation the 'less is more' principle really does apply.

Checklist : Customer relationship management

What processes do you have in place to monitor, collate and respond to your customer persona's changing needs and expectations?

Have you balanced financial, marketing, innovation and process to feed your marketing performance improvements?

How will you continuously innovate your customers' experience and measure the impact for continuous improvement?

What are your baseline measures for Return on Marketing Investment and how are you currently performing?

What will you do next to improve your Return on Marketing Investment?

Is your digital dashboard focused on enhancing your customer relationship management?

12.2 IMPROVE : INNOVATE : ADAPTING BEHAVIOURS

Helping Your Organisation To View Social Media Strategically

Modern organisations of all sizes need to become 'social businesses'. The old model of large marketing departments has gone. Social media now provides the opportunity for all levels of your organisation to create an audience for your business.

Alongside your broadcast marketing the individual's in a social business create their own audience.

The organically built audience that follows a real human being in an organisation will have more trust and loyalty towards the individual and company. Accumulatively these audiences add up to a very important resource.

The first step towards taking your organisation strategically into social media is to accept that willing and able staff are your best advocates and can be trusted online with the right help and support.

Here are the steps you need to take:

1   Identify a core team to steer and monitor the social media development.

2   Decide what you're trying to achieve through the social media - this might be visits to a certain webpage or a greater understanding of your processes. REMEMBER social media is not just about selling.

3   Agree Key Performance Indicators (KPI) and timescales. REMEMBER the best results from social media come over time, there are few quick wins.

4   Discover the current digital extroverts in your company (they may only be doing it personally at the moment) and invite them to help. They will need to be involved in the planning stages so they understand the big picture and see the part they play in it. Not everyone will want to go online in your business and that's fine, encourage the ones that do and let them encourage others in time.

5   As a group complete our Social Business Model (see image) - each member of staff should be targeting a specific audience according to the role they play in the organisation.

Directors and senior staff may be targeting politicians, fellow CEOs or other influential people. Finance staff may target business gurus for research purposes. Remote staff or location based staff can target residents of these locations.

6   After the group has completed the over-arching model then individuals should focus on their section (see image) to complete the content Rule of Thirds.

7   The team needs to agree a common approach to going online e.g. the initials of the company at the end of their Twitter handle, profile and image guidelines. Keep them simple and memorable, most importantly involve the team in producing the guidelines and they'll be more likely to follow them.

8   Don't be afraid to try things out online. The nature of social media is that everything changes fast - a few years ago there were no such things as business pages on Facebook!

9   Manage expectations of the target audiences, let them know these are business accounts and not monitored 24 hours a day.

10   The core team monitors the KPIs and reports back on a weekly basis to the whole company celebrating success.

At this stage in the building of a digital marketing plan or strategy our attention should turn to another type of customer, our internal customer. Others in our organisation, or agency suppliers and consultants, all have a potentially significant part to play in the development, launch and ongoing delivery of our ideas and plans.

There are key considerations for your internal digital marketing communications: technology, process and systems; people as part of the digital marketing mix.

Internal web sites, or intranets, can revolutionise internal communications. The base principles of internet web sites follow those for intranets. They can help employees feel informed and part of the organisation, improve productivity and reduce inefficiency. If kept regularly updated, the intranet can ensure all employees have the latest information in a consistent manner whilst reducing paper and print costs normally associated with printed employee newsletters.

The intranet or equivalent internal information sharing platform allows the marketer to provide early campaign briefings to those who need to be informed prior to public launch. These might include new product introductions, sales and marketing or business development campaigns, industry news and strategic internal announcements.

The more advanced intranets allow for collaborative project working and can act as a company archive resource. If the requirement is to extend collaboration beyond the internal team and integrate others into the mix then an extranet (intranet with password protected access to selected others outside of the organisation) can be invaluable.

Extranets are another tool for sales and marketing and the technology required to support relationships with sales channels (distributors, agents, wholesalers, retailers, dealers) and even VIP customers. The benefit of an extranet is that customer-specific pricing, materials and support can be provided in their own ring-fenced areas, quite distinct to the publicly available information on the main website.

Marketing information systems, which are discussed later, also come into the internal communications mix as a central hub of data collection and manipulation. The more people and departments who can be directly involved in the collection and collation of such data (customer, market, trends, financial, subjective) the better as it provides vital customer and market insight that informs great decision making.

Companies and their marketers, should remember that digital marketing must inherently link with existing offline sales and marketing activity, supporting real world campaigns, business development and sales visits as well as potentially warming up new markets for growth into new sectors or countries.

Some businesses see their CEO or MD as the face of the organisation and this may or may not be an appropriate decision, depending on the individual and the target persona.

If you are Virgin then Richard Branson as the face of the organisation is appropriate. A growing local company with diverse target personas may benefit more from having someone operational or more readily accessible as part of their brand profile. The decision should be driven by customer/persona perception. Who do they want to see and engage with? Who are they most interested in? If it is to provide a fascinating behind the scenes, 'fly on the wall' insight then someone operational would be appropriate. If your CEO or MD is a charismatic and relevant individual who will motivate and inspire the persona then they could be the most appropriate.

Take ego out of the decision, focus on customer intimacy and an innate knowledge of what the persona feels is best and you will find the best fit.

Another key use of others in your organisation as part of the marketing mix is they could be a regular and perhaps specialist feed of content to fuel the digital marketing campaigns or plans.

Marketing should not be left to the marketers. There will be pockets of excellent content opportunity around the organisation and it is vital to tap into this to ensure the outputs are relevant, authentic and balanced. Transparent organisations who document their inner workings (without giving away commercial secrets of course) are those stealing maximum share of voice in the chaotic digital noise.

The delivery driver with a smartphone is much more likely to have great content opportunities for Instagram than the marketer tied to a desk. The technical guru deep in the R&D lab is more likely to have specialist insight and golden nuggets of information for their technical counterparts in customer organisations than the marketer focused solely on campaigns and promotions.

It is all about collaboration and allowing the people in the organisation to self-nominate and contribute appropriately.

Brand and communication guidelines are vital to ensure boundaries are set and agreed and within which anything goes. Give freedom with carefully planned limits and you open up creativity. Open the flood gates and let anything go and the marketer's role turns more into a police officer for the brand.

Internal communication is at the heart of successful public digital marketing activities. Consider your peers and colleagues as customer and create a persona(s) for them too.

With the plethora of analytics and insights, digital marketers have the opportunity to review and adapt behaviour and plans not only in monthly or quarterly reviews, but every day, to the point of real-time if they so wish.

Data analysis, the turning of insights and information into intelligence to inform great decision making, should be considered as guiding corrective action on a day to day, hour to hour basis. This is especially crucial for when running campaigns for market research, A/B testing or for time-bound, short-term sales and marketing.

The ability to monitor and adjust, down to the granular level of an individual tweet, ensures that the alert marketer has the opportunity to drive increasing return on investment in all of their activities online.

Individual snippets of data can be useful but better still is the monitoring of trends.

To see a steady trend, either positive or negative, is highly valuable information which can clearly emphasise the amount of change in behaviour or resources required by the marketer.

This is where customer behaviours and needs can be shared across the organisation to not only improve and adapt online behaviour but that in the physical world too. Sharing patterns with sales, business development and customer service colleagues can help to integrate and gel the experience the company gives to the customer. In turn this should stimulate those colleagues to share back their observations, which can also be tested.

Checklist : Adapting behaviours

Adapting you and your team's behaviours is even more important than the outputs of your content and activities so how are you measuring ongoing improvements?

What Key Performance Indicators are in place for ongoing performance measurement and improvement?

How will you create and a deliver a continuous improvement training and development program for yourself and others?

Where and when will you share how you and your people are developing and adapting behaviours to become ever more customer outcome focused?

12.3 IMPROVE : INNOVATE : LEAVING A LEGACY

The internet is certainly here to stay. In At its beginnings, in 1996, information was key. By 1999 speed of transactions and the dot.com boom threatened the entire online business model and investment poured back into traditional businesses as online businesses quickly became out of favour. Those organisations with the sound strategic business models, rooted in proven business practice survived and have grown significantly to become key players in the global marketplace. The lead example of course being the global behemoth, Amazon.

Recent improvements in connection speeds (over 100 MB and accelerating) with the growth of 4G coverage and exciting new mobile internet applications has led Microsoft to declare they believe the future will be in intelligent devices that aid the user to control broad aspects of their lives from their intelligent home and vehicle to interactive mobile multimedia infotainment... the internet of things.

The rapid emergence of smart electric vehicles, powered by the Tesla strategy, will drive this growing marketplace in the coming years.

New devices and an ever growing variety of mobile applications have driven overall growth. Instant messaging growth continues to astound onlookers and the surge of smartphone apps and widgets provides significant opportunities for enhanced engagement and stimulation of loyalty in some target customer segments. The always-on and immediacy expectations of customers poses new challenges for marketers offering customer service.

It is anticipated that we are currently on the cusp of witnessing one of the greatest revolutions since the printing press. Persistently, mobile technologies are at the cutting edge of this curve of change as we move towards the ubiquitous internet of things where marketers will not only have to consider humans as their customers but machines and objects too.

Maslow's Hierarchy of Needs and Social Networking

Maslow's Hierarchy of Needs might translate into the realities of day to day marketing operations in many businesses.

Self actualisation - *"I feel like I'm doing a great job because my marketing makes lots of noise. I don't know which bit of marketing works well because I don't measure anything but we are noisy so it makes me feel good and something must be working. So, friendly marketing consultant, give me more of the same."*

Esteem - *"We have lots of visitors to our website every month so I can bask in the glory of success even though I am not sure where they go on the site, who they are, what they are interested in or how much business this turns into. So, friendly marketing consultant, give me a glossy website that looks better and more up to date."*

Social - *"We've got thousands of followers on our social networks and this is great because we can sell to them, raise our brand awareness, keep pushing our special offers and generally promote, promote, promote, although we aren't sure if they are actually listening. So, friendly marketing consultant, I want you to run a campaign to get us more followers because surely that'll turn everything we do into new business leads and sales opportunities."*

OK. So here is where we stop in our tracks and take a deep breath. The reality is, as Maslow would likely confirm, you should really start with the building blocks at the engine room of the hierarchy of needs. You need a strong competitive position and to do this you need a strong financial position and awareness. You need leadership and appropriate operations. You need a suitable level of sales and marketing resource and positioning and you need, above all, a strategy.

Without the building blocks that look after the physiology and safety of your business you are going to spend time, money and resources doing more of the same chaos that may well be holding you back.

So yes, we can help you to deliver your digital desires and sales and marketing goals but first, we would like to challenge your financials, your priorities, your leadership, your operations, your sales and marketing and help you to create a solid, robust strategy to ensure everything we then do, will help you achieve your business objectives.

Another key tip for stardom and already proving successful in business to business applications is synthesis of the words 'Pod' and 'broadcast', in the digital tool Podcast.

Derived from the first scripting codes that were developed for the portable Apple iPod branded media/music player invented in 2004, podcasts (and their video counterpart the 'vodcast') are seeing exponential growth as consumer and business brands see this rich media engagement as a fundamental method for imparting their messages and stimulating two way engagement with customers and prospects.

The rapid growth of celebrity bloggers, vloggers and YouTubers are clear evidence of the thirst of the world's online population for content that is both informative, educative and a glimpse of the real worlds of such people and their businesses.

As we see increasing focus on how to improve customer intimacy it's likely we will see this emerge in the form of virtual reality and virtual worlds.

It is also likely we will see a continued development of virtual worlds with an amalgamation not only of the virtual gaming experience into the real world interactions of gamers but also with more mainstream and business-focused applications.

A virtual world is an online community that interacts with one another through a simulated world. The term today has become synonymous with interactive 3D virtual environments, where the users take the form of avatars visible to others graphically. These avatars are usually depicted as textual, two-dimensional, or three-dimensional graphical representations, although other forms are possible.

Segmentation for Personalisation not Generalisation

Segmentation is, by nature, stereotyping. It is the grouping together of people by common needs, behaviours, location, product interest, age, demographics, millions of other things and often a combination of all of the above.

To the untrained eye this could be perceived as stereotyping, leading to generalisations and unhelpful marketing or communication activities.

Nothing should be further from the truth. Authentic and well-intended segmentation should lead not to generalisation but to personalisation. The more accurate the definition of each segment, the potentially more accurate the engagement with them. With the right intelligence and interpretation of their behaviours and needs, the more accurate the ongoing communication and conversations.

With improvements in these areas, the result should be longer and higher quality, sustained relationships leading to mutually beneficial outcomes. More value to the customer and more profit to the business.

We have discussed throughout, that there is a sound argument for considering digital marketing as just another element of the overall strategic marketing plan for an organisation.

Digital marketing should therefore be included within business goals and objectives, a situational review both internal and external, and of course a SWOT analysis.

Strategic development should include investment and resource commitment and market and product positioning in a similar way to a traditional marketing plan. As part of the strategy an organisation must decide on the fundamental role that its digital marketing will take in the growth of its business.

Following agreement across the business that the digital strategy is appropriate for the organisation the next stage is implementation. The organisation needs to commit resource not only to the initial development and launch but importantly to the fulfilment, customer response and service, any necessary restructuring and re-engineering processes.

The internet is here to stay. At its beginnings, in 1996, information was key. By 1999 speed of transactions and the dot.com boom threatened the entire e-business model and investment poured back into traditional businesses as e-business quickly became out of favour. Those organisations with the sound strategic business models, rooted in proven business practice survived and have grown significantly to become key players in the global marketplace.

We must all learn from this. It's not just about your choice of social media today, the number of followers you have, or the next big thing. It is about ensuring you have a clear long term strategy, carefully choreographed customer journey, one eye on the competition and a hunger to learn something new in the exciting world of digital marketing, each and every day.

Keeping Up With The Social Networking

Try stopping and starting your social media following, engagement and conversations and you see quickly that things can quickly grind to a halt and how does that look from the customers' perspective?

Stop and it stalls, restart and the conversation and successes and advocacy resumes. There is a clear link between activity and outcomes. It's not simply a 'do more and you get more' but it's pretty close.

We have been running a test over recent weeks with a client's Twitter account. We've been doing the normal type of publishing and conversations but have been stopping and starting the amount of proactive engagement and following of other marketers. Each time we stop there's a clear and fast slowing down of activity and each time we begin again it is like turning on a tap of warm water and everything begins to flow.

So the lesson we can share with confidence and some evidence is that in social networking you get what you give.

Here are some ideas for how to maintain the initial momentum so you steadily build great up a return on investment of your time and energy when you are networking:

1. Dedicate specific time each day and every day. This is part of your working life not an addition to it
2. Think about checking your social media when you check your emails as you are likely to be in the same frame of mind
3. Prioritise your networks so you focus appropriate time where your customers are and where they are most likely to respond
4. Get lots of little wins. Make sure you set lots of short term targets, each one contributing to the greater digital marketing strategy
5. Measure everything you do down to individual posts and

tweets so you learn quickly what works and what to avoid next time

6. Follow, share and like more than those who follow, share and like you to ensure you are highly engaged and 'out there'

7. Balance research with promotion so you listen and learn as much as you talk and market

8. Get others onboard and share the workload, with a consistent output and style but some level of individuality

9. Take days off so you come back refreshed and ready for more

10. Make it mobile so you can social network wherever you are to save time and prevent yourself forgetting the great ideas and opportunities that pop up during the day

How do you plan to keep your social networking momentum going?

Checklist : Leaving a legacy

How will you keep to date with emerging trends and new technological opportunities?

What market and marketing information will you need to continuously feed into your innovations and future thinking?

How will you consistently and continuously maintain momentum with your digital marketing and social networking?

Have you successfully integrated your digital marketing into your wider business development activities and operations?

What clear legacy are you planning to leave behind as you exit your first phase of digital marketing activities?

Celebrate that you have made it this far. You are already so far ahead of your competitors because you have a strategy and a plan... good luck with your next steps....t

ABOUT THE AUTHOR

Neil Wilkins is a Psychology graduate, Marketing Consultant and Fellow of Cambridge Marketing College. He teaches Chartered Institute of Marketing qualification courses and has over 30 years of strategic and practical experience in marketing across sectors as diverse as law, manufacturing, telecoms and financial services.

He is founder of Viper Marketing, a communications consultancy with offices in UK, UAE and Egypt and has been active in digital marketing and social media since launching his first website in 1994.

www.neilwilkins.online
@neilwilkinsx

www.ingramcontent.com/pod-product-compliance
Lightning Source LLC
Chambersburg PA
CBHW071449220526
45472CB00003B/730